'Pastry is a dying craft. It takes time and care to make a dessert or cake to be proud of and this is too demanding for some people. I have known James for many years, particularly through my chef friends and Roux Scholarship judges, David Nicholls and Gary Rhodes, who I know to be demanding, uncompromising professionals who accept nothing but the best. They found in James, a very knowledgeable Pastry Chef and master craftsman. I have always enjoyed James' desserts. I recall in particular tasting his outstanding Pink Peppercorn & Passion Fruit Eton Mess as well as his dessert of Smoked Chocolate Pavé with Yuzu Ganache, Miso & Peanut Butter Crunch. On both occasions, I had not even finished my plate, I had to find him in the kitchen and congratulate him, for I knew it was James and recognized his very delicate touch. We all find inspiration in our peers and their special, unique qualities. James' desserts deliver a kind of firework in your mouth, incredible but still delicate, light and delicious. The proof of a good dessert is when at the end of a meal, you are tempted and excited all over again, if not even more than for the courses that have gone before. He is a master not only of classic techniques but fusion-not-confusion. His mastery is in fact achieving that perfect balance, an authority in his craft that is set alight with his flair and open-minded approach. A simply stunning pastry chef.'

MICHEL ROUX, OBE

'The culinary world is full of flavoursome surprises, the majority including foods, with the remainder often embracing the skills to source the young who hold such a wealth of talent. James joined my team many, many years ago as an eager young man wanting to look, learn and discover sweet foodie characters amongst dishes, always hungry and itching to add his own personality to the finished plate. There are countless who pass us by unnoticed but James' raw skills stood out and, like many a dish, he required simply the fine-tuning and palatable balance to set him on his way. This young man was a joy to work with and teach, the enthusiasm so apparent and strong, with his skills and initiative improving as each day passed. The following pages of words, ideas and dishes in this book tell the story of Campbell's numerous culinary experiences around the world, all within everyone's reach while never dispossessing his masters' tutoring. I congratulate James and send him my culinary best wishes of lasting success for many years to come.'

GARY RHODES, OBE

JAPANESE
PÂTISSERIE

JAPANESE PÂTISSERIE

Exploring the beautiful and delicious
fusion of East meets West

JAMES CAMPBELL
photography by Mowie Kay

RYLAND PETERS & SMALL
LONDON • NEW YORK

Dedication

To the industry, thank you for giving me so much and to my incredible family, thank you for allowing me to put so much in.

Senior designer Megan Smith
Editor Alice Sambrook
Head of production
 Patricia Harrington
Art director Leslie Harrington
Editorial director Julia Charles
Publisher Cindy Richards
Food stylist James Campbell
Assistants Alex Laverick
 and Jon Jones
Prop stylist Tony Hutchinson
Indexer Vanessa Bird

First published in 2017 by
Ryland Peters & Small
20–21 Jockey's Fields,
London WC1R 4BW
and
341 E 116th St, New York NY 10029
www.rylandpeters.com

10 9 8 7 6 5 4 3 2 1

Text copyright © James Campbell 2017

Design and photographs copyright
© Ryland Peters & Small 2017

ISBN: 978-1-84975-810-9

Printed in China

Notes

All desserts which are frozen as part of their construction should be fully defrosted before serving.

Both British (Metric) and American (Imperial plus US cups) measurements are included in these recipes for your convenience, however it is important to work with one set of measurements and not alternate between the two.

Where very small measurements occur, they have been provided in grams where there is no suitable imperial conversion.

All spoon and cup measurements are level unless otherwise specified.

All butter is unsalted unless otherwise specified.

Eggs are medium (UK) or large (US), unless otherwise specified. Uncooked or partially cooked eggs should not be served to the very old, frail, young children, pregnant women or those with compromised immune systems.

When a recipe calls for the grated zest of citrus fruit, buy unwaxed fruit and wash well before using. If you can only find treated fruit, scrub well in warm soapy water before using.

Recipes were tested using a fan oven. Adjust temperatures according to the manufacturer's instructions.

CONTENTS

INTRODUCTION

As a wee boy growing up in Scotland, I was lucky enough to always be surrounded by fresh produce and great home cooking. From sitting eating home-grown raw rhubarb in my uncle Harry's back garden (with a little pot of sugar to dip it in, of course), to my nana's apple crumbles and my mother's clootie dumpling, my awareness of and interest in good food was sparked at a young age.

I left school at the age of 17 and was fortunate enough to begin my career in Cameron House, a stunning 5-star hotel on the banks of Loch Lomond. After 6 months in the main kitchen, I moved into the pastry kitchen and my love and passion for pâtisserie began. I went on to work in some great kitchens all over Scotland, and eventually moved to London in 2000.

At 24 years-old I was given the opportunity by Gary Rhodes to become Head Pastry Chef at his Michelin-starred Rhodes in the Square restaurant. Apart from a short 18-month spell in Australia, I have spent the majority of my career in London. A particular highlight was my time as Head Pastry Chef of the Mandarin Oriental Hotel, where I had 4 very hard but happy years under the guidance of Lisa Phillips and David Nicholls.

Having a family spurred me on to take my career in a slightly new direction. I am now loving working for Marks & Spencer, where my food-focused brain is being used in a different but exciting and more strategic way to research and oversee the development of new products.

This book has been a joy to work on. My professional career has taken me to some of the best kitchens in the UK and around the world, and I have always had a particular appreciation for East Asian and South-East Asian cooking. The precision and attention to detail of Japanese culture has always fascinated me, but I think I truly fell in love with Japanese cuisine after I visited the country almost 3 years ago on a mission to scout out new ideas for M&S. The celebration of seasonality and genuine care and attention to detail in everything from the preparation of the food to the service and considerate nature of the Japanese people absolutely blew my mind. I have been obsessed with Japan and experimenting with Japanese ingredients in my cooking ever since.

The thing that really impressed me about Japan and Tokyo, specifically, was the stunning fusion of traditional Japanese flavours with the French pâtisserie-style recipes, which gives simply beautiful and delicious results. This book has been an outlet for combining my lifelong passion for classic French pâtisserie with my new passion for contemporary Japanese flavours. I have also woven in some other exotic ingredients that just worked beautifully together and were commonplace in many of the Japanese menus that I saw when I was over there.

I am very proud of this book and I truly hope you enjoy the recipes, I have tried to work these magical flavours into formats that won't be too unfamiliar. Please experiment and allow them to inspire you to create your own culinary adventures.

James Campbell

SPECIALIST INGREDIENTS & EQUIPMENT

I have compiled a list of some of the more unusual ingredients and equipment used throughout this book to help you get started. This list includes Japanese ingredients as well as a few high-end pâtisserie ingredients. Some of these are widely available in stores, others can be found online or in specialist Japanese stores. There are some great tips on my list of suppliers (page 176) and don't forget to check out the flavour wheel on page 11, which gives you a quick flavour profile for unfamiliar ingredients.

FRUITS

YUZU: a perfumed citrus fruit, the flavour is a mixture of lemon, lime and grapefruit. I use yuzu purée or juice for many recipes, which is easy to find when the whole fruits are not in season.

KUMQUAT: originally from China, the kumquat is a common ingredient in Japanese cooking. The small, bitter citrus fruits need to be cooked slowly to break down their tough skins. Their flavour is stunning when cooked properly.

KINKAN: a type of kumquat commonly used in Japan.

MOMO FRUIT: a type of Japanese peach, quite similar to its European cousin, with similar properties but a hybrid of both white and yellow peaches.

SUDACHI FRUIT: similar in look and smell to a lime but much more sour, commonly used in both sweet and savoury dishes in Japan.

SPICES & FLAVOURINGS

CHERRY BLOSSOM: also called sakura, the famous short-lived cherry blossom season 'Hanami' (meaning viewing of the flowers) is highly celebrated in Japan. You can buy salt-cured cherry blossoms that need careful cleaning, stalks removing and then soaking in sweetened water to draw out the salt. You can also find freeze-dried cherry blossom flakes and cherry blossom essence online.

TONKA BEANS: from a flowering tree in the pea family, tonka beans have a complex heavily perfumed flavour, with notes of vanilla, cherry, almonds and a slightly spicy quality. They are often used as a vanilla replacement, and work very well with raspberry and milk chocolate. In very large doses (100 times more than what I use here) they can be toxic, so are illegal in some countries.

MATCHA POWDER: a Japanese tea powder which features a lot throughout this book. It is similar in taste and appearance to standard green tea, but the process of making it gives a more refined finish and only the best leaves are used. It is high in antioxidants and gives a beautiful colour and flavour.

SAKE: a Japanese rice wine made from rice that has been polished to remove the bran, it is then fermented to make a clear alcoholic drink. There are two basic types of sake: Futsu-shu, the ordinary or standard version and Tokutei meisho-shu, the premium version. Much like choosing a cooking wine, I would go for the ordinary or standard sake for these recipes. I also occasionally use a sparkling sake.

PINK PEPPERCORNS: widely available in most stores, these are mildly spiced but very perfumed, therefore ideal in bakes and desserts. They work exceptionally well with perfumed citrus flavours such as passion fruit or yuzu fruit.

SANSHO PEPPER: despite its name, sansho pepper is actually more of an earthy, tangy spice with a hint of lemon. It is closely related to Sichuan pepper. The best sansho is green in colour.

TAHINI: a paste made from toasted ground sesame seeds, tahini is now widely available in most stores. Much like peanut butter it has a rich, nutty flavour which pairs very well with chocolate. This is also widely used in Middle Eastern cooking too.

KOSHIAN: a sweet adzuki bean paste that can be bought pre-made or easily made using the recipe provided on page 19. Also sometimes called tsubuan, it is a very common addition in Japanese desserts. Adzuki in its natural state is a very savoury flavour so the sweetness needs to be balanced carefully.

MISO: a seasoned soya bean fermented paste, this comes in brown, red, yellow or white. I use white miso for nearly all the recipes in this book. Also known as 'sweet' or 'mellow' miso, it is fermented for the least time and so has the most delicate flavour.

HIGH-END PÂTISSERIE

GELATINE: it is important to note that gelatine comes in two sizes: smaller domestic leaves (available in most stores, used by home-cooks) and larger commercial sheets (mostly used by professional chefs). I have provided both options in the recipes but make sure you use the right amount for the type of gelatine you buy.

GELLAN GUM: a vegetable gelling agent that gives structure and also helps viscosity. You will need some scales that can measure in small increments to get the precise quantities needed. It is also usually mixed with a small amount of sugar before being used.

ACIDIC YOGURT POWDER: a bakeable powder that can also be eaten in its natural form, it adds an incredible lactic flavour to desserts.

CITRIC ACID: this is useful for many things, I have used it to stop jelly turning to jam when making a classic pâte de fruit (see page 90).

INVERTED SUGAR: used predominantly as a stabilizer, trimoline is the most common type but liquid glucose can also be substituted if you can't find it.

PECTIN: a naturally occuring thickening agent when heated with sugar, it is brilliant in jams and jellies.

EQUIPMENT

SILICONE MOULDS: several desserts in this book require the use of silicone moulds, especially in the Large Cakes & Gâteaux chapter (pages 72–101). This will either be a large mould or a smaller 'insert' mould that will make the inner layer of a dessert. You don't have to use exactly the same shape if you can't find it but be guided by the serving amount and choose one that holds a similar volume. Often, you can use a cake pan or even a small plastic tub instead, if the shape is simillar. Standard shaped silicone moulds are widely available in baking stores but see suppliers (page 176) for information on where to order the specialist shapes I use online. I find www.silikomart.com have a great selection.

ESPUMA GUN: also known as a siphon, I use this to make a micro sponge garnish but it is also a very useful piece of kit to have for making interesting foams and sauces. You will also need a polystyrene cup and microwave for the micro sponges.

SPRAY GUN: a pâtisserie food-grade spray gun is useful if you want to make decorative sprays from scratch. However, you can just as easily use a can of store-bought coloured chocolate velvet spray.

COOK'S BLOWTORCH: Useful for giving a charred finish on a few items throughout the book.

VACK PACK MACHINE: a professional piece of kit, useful for many things and simple to operate. I have included an alternative method if you don't have one.

FLAVOUR WHEEL

Use this flavour wheel to help you identify the flavour attributes of unfamiliar ingredients. Once you understand the flavours, you can mix and match them to create your own unique combinations. This understanding also comes in handy when certain ingredients are unavailable so that you can correctly choose a substitute with the same basic flavour. For example, using sharp lemons instead of yuzu or a pinch of sea salt instead of miso. Some ingredients with complex flavours fall into up to three categories.

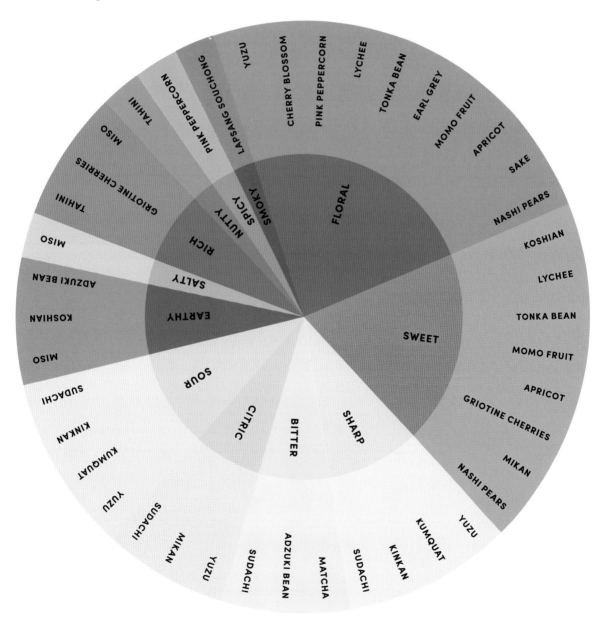

BASIC RECIPES
CHOUX PASTRY

Choux pastry or pâte à choux is a light, airy pastry used in many traditional pâtisserie items from profiteroles/cream puffs, to éclairs, rings for a Paris-brest or even savoury gougères. Unusually for pastry it needs to be cooked over heat which has perhaps given it an unfair reputation as being difficult to master. If you follow these instructions carefully, it is actually fairly simple to put together. It should come out of the oven golden and crisp on the outside, puffed up and almost hollow on the inside, ready to be cooled and then stuffed with a delicious filling.

145 ml/scant ⅔ cup whole milk
145 g/scant 1¼ sticks butter
½ teaspoon table salt
½ teaspoon caster/superfine sugar
1 teaspoon pure vanilla extract
145 g/1 cup white/strong bread flour
4 eggs

MAKES APPROX.
500 G/18 OZ.

Combine the milk and butter with 145 ml/scant ⅔ cup water in a small saucepan. Set over medium heat and bring to the boil.

Once boiling, immediately stir in the salt, sugar and vanilla extract until combined. Remove the pan from the heat and add the flour all in one go. Beat vigorously with a wooden spoon or silicone spatula until the mixture comes together into a smooth ball of paste that leaves the sides of the pan.

Put the pan back on the heat and let the flour cook out for 5 minutes, stirring to make sure the mixture does not stick to the bottom of the pan.

Remove the pan from heat and gradually but firmly beat the eggs into the hot pastry, one by one, until fully combined and the mixture is smooth, soft and glossy. When you lift the spoon up the mixture should drop off when lightly shaken.

Your choux paste is now ready to be transferred to a piping/pastry bag and used. I will normally instruct you to brush with a little beaten egg before baking to give the pastry a glossy shine when baked.

SWEET SHORTCRUST PASTRY

This rich, sweet pastry is the perfect basic recipe for all the tarts in the tarts chapter (see pages 56–71). Any pastry chef will tell you that the secret to good pastry is to keep everything cold. Cold butter, cold hands and cold work surfaces for rolling out.

270 g/2½ sticks butter
180 g/1 cup minus 1½ tablespoons caster/granulated sugar
2 UK large/US extra-large eggs
540 g/scant 4¼ cups plain/all-purpose flour

MAKES ENOUGH FOR 2 LARGE TARTS OR 8 INDIVIDUAL

Put the butter and sugar in a large mixing bowl and cream together using a wooden spoon or a hand-held electric whisk. You don't need to mix for too long, just until well combined.

Add the eggs gradually, one by one, and beat until smooth and completely incorporated. Finally, gently fold in the flour until just combined, being careful not to over-work the dough.

Form the dough into a ball and wrap in clingfilm/plastic wrap and chill in the refrigerator for 30 minutes. It is important to chill the pastry properly so that it is easy to handle and won't shrink when baked.

When ready to use, roll the pastry out on a lightly floured surface to the required thickness before using to line your tart pan.

CHOCOLATE SHORTCRUST PASTRY

A very useful and gorgeous chocolate version of classic tart pastry with a lovely bitter edge that comes from using extra-dark cocoa powder. You can mix and match this pastry with any of the tart fillings as you prefer.

270 g/2½ sticks butter
180 g/1 cup minus 1½ tablespoons caster/granulated sugar
2 UK large/US extra-large eggs
500 g/3¾ cups plain/all-purpose flour
40 g/⅓ cup extra-dark cocoa powder

MAKES ENOUGH FOR 2 LARGE TARTS OR 8 INDIVIDUAL

Put the butter and sugar in a large mixing bowl and cream together using a wooden spoon or a hand-held electric whisk. You don't need to mix for too long, just until well combined.

Add the eggs gradually, one by one, and beat until smooth and completely incorporated. Finally, gently fold in the flour and cocoa powder until just combined, being careful not to over-work the dough.

Form the dough into a ball and wrap in clingfilm/plastic wrap and chill in the refrigerator for 30 minutes. It is important to chill the pastry properly so that it is easy to handle and won't shrink when baked.

When ready to use, roll the pastry out on a lightly floured surface to the required thickness before using to line your tart pan.

CRÈME PÂTISSIÈRE

Also known as crème pat or pastry cream, this luxurious, thick filling can be used in all sorts of pâtisserie goodies. Once you have mastered the basic recipe you can add flavourings such as matcha powder or chocolate.

300 ml/generous 1¼ cups
    whole milk
a pinch of salt
seeds from 1 vanilla pod/
    bean
4 egg yolks
25 g/¼ cup cornflour/
    cornstarch
75 g/⅓ cup plus 2 teaspoons
    caster/superfine sugar

MAKES APPROX.
500 G/18 OZ.

Put the milk, salt and vanilla seeds in a heavy saucepan and bring to the boil over a low-medium heat.

Meanwhile, in a separate bowl, whisk together the egg yolks, cornflour/cornstarch and caster/superfine sugar with a balloon whisk. Slowly pour the hot milk into the egg mixture and whisk until fully combined and thickened.

Pour everything back into the pan and return to the stove over medium heat, whisking constantly until the cornflour/cornstarch has been cooked out completely and the mixture is thickened and bubbling.

Transfer the crème pâtissière to a bowl and whisk occasionally until completely cool. Cover with clingfilm/plastic wrap and keep refrigerated.

CRÈME DIPLOMAT

A delicious cream with all the flavour of crème pâtissière, but much lighter in texture. Please note, it is best to prepare this crème just before you plan to serve.

the cooled crème pâtissière
    from the recipe above
100 ml/scant ½ cup double/
    heavy cream

MAKES APPROX.
600 G/21 OZ.

Prepare the crème pâtissière following the instructions above and let cool completely. When cool, give it a final stir to make sure it is smooth.

Gently whisk in a little of the double/heavy cream, being careful not to over-whip. Add the remainder of the double/heavy cream gradually and whip to the desired thickness.

Adding a little at a time in this way should ensure that you do not get any lumps. Refrigerate and serve straight away or within a couple of hours if possible.

ALMOND MILK & CHERRY BLOSSOM JAM

This versatile recipe stores well in the refrigerator and works beautifully
as a conserve that can be served in many different ways.

300 ml/1¼ cups
  unsweetened almond milk
2½ tablespoons caster/
  granulated sugar
50 g/½ cup ground almonds
2–3 drops of cherry blossom
  flavouring (available online)
gellan gum: 1.5% of total
  weight, mixed with enough
  caster/granulated sugar to
  disperse (approx. 1 tbsp)
a little extra almond milk for
  blending the jam

scales that can measure small
  increments

MAKES APPROX.
1 SMALL JAR

Put the almond milk, caster/granulated sugar and ground almonds in a saucepan, stir together and bring to boiling point. Remove the pan from the heat and set aside to let the flavours infuse for around 20 minutes.

Strain the mixture through a sieve, weigh the amount of liquid you are left with and then weigh out 1.5% of the total weight in gellan (for example, if the mixture is 300 g/10 ½ oz. in total, it would be 4.5 g/3/4 oz. of gellan). Mix the gellan with a little caster/granulated sugar then put the milk back in the saucepan over a high heat and bring to the boil. Add 2–3 drops of cherry blossom flavouring to taste, then whisk in the gellan and continue to whisk until completely incorporated.

Pour the mixture into a tray or container lined with clingfilm/plastic wrap and allow to cool and set completely. Once totally cooled, blitz in the blender (or with the stick blender), adding a little extra almond milk to achieve the desired consistency; if the milk seems a little lumpy, just keep blending and scraping down the sides as you do so and these lumps will disperse. Transfer the jam to a sterilized jar or container, cover and refrigerate until required.

MATCHA CURD

This recipe is a real delight served with the kouign-amann (see page 50)
or as an accompaniment to scones (see page 54) for afternoon tea.

150 ml/²⁄₃ cup whole milk
50 g/scant ¼ cup condensed
  milk
20 g/3 tablespoons matcha
  powder
4 egg yolks
2 eggs
50 g/¼ cup caster/granulated
  sugar
50 g/3½ tablespoons butter,
  diced

MAKES APPROX.
250 G/8 OZ.

Put the whole milk, condensed milk and matcha powder in a saucepan and stir together. Place the pan over high heat and bring the mixture to the boil.

In a separate bowl, mix together the egg yolks, whole eggs and caster/granulated sugar. Strain the hot milk into the bowl with the egg and sugar mixture, whisking continuously to fully combine. Transfer everything back to the pan over medium heat and bring to the boil, whisking constantly.

Simmer while whisking for about 2–3 minutes until the mixture thickens. Remove from the heat and transfer the curd to a bowl. Add the diced butter and stir every few minutes until all of the butter has melted and is fully incorporated. If the mixture looks a little curdled (which can happen and is quite normal) blitz in a food processor or with a stick blender to properly emulsify.

Transfer the matcha curd to a sterilized jar or container and once cool, refrigerate until required.

KOSHIAN PASTE

You can buy this sweet adzuki bean paste from most specialist Japanese stores but in case you cannot find it or want to make your own, use the recipe below.

200 g/7 oz. dried adzuki
   beans
100 g/½ cup caster/
   granulated sugar

MAKES APPROX.
80 G/3 OZ.

Soak the adzuki beans overnight in water to soften.

Drain and rinse the beans, then place in a large saucepan with the caster/granulated sugar and cover with fresh water. Bring the beans to the boil then reduce the heat to a simmer.

Cover the pan and simmer gently for around 60–90 minutes, topping up with water as needed. Cook until the beans are soft and break apart between your fingers quite easily.

Drain the beans and blend to a smooth purée in a food processor. Pass the purée through a fine-mesh sieve/strainer to make sure it is as smooth as possible.

KUMQUAT & KINKAN MARMALADE

This fresh marmalade is quite soft-set and loose in texture but it is utterly delicious; if you want a warmer taste, you can add about 60 ml/¼ cup of Japanese whisky at the end of the cooking time.

150 g/5¼ oz. kumquats
150 g/5¼ oz. kinkan fruit
freshly squeezed juice of
   1 lemon
450 g/2¼ cups preserving
   sugar

muslin/cheesecloth and kitchen
   string/twine
sterilized Kilner/Mason jar

MAKES APPROX.
1 SMALL JAR

Cut all the fruits in half and squeeze over a sieve/strainer to catch the pips/seeds and membrane, reserving the juices in a separate bowl. Put the contents of the sieve/strainer into the muslin/cheesecloth and tie up with the kitchen string/twine.

Put the lemon juice and preserving sugar into a large heavy-based saucepan. Add 600 ml/generous 2½ cups water, the reserved juices squeezed from the fruits and the tied up muslin/cheesecloth. Bring to the boil and simmer uncovered for around 1½ hours until reduced and thickened, skimming often to remove any foam from the surface.

Meanwhile, put a plate in the freezer ready to test the thickness of the marmalade. When you think that it's ready, put a spoonful of marmalade on the very cold plate and push your finger through. If it wrinkles instead of flowing back to fill the gap then it is ready. If not, simmer for a little longer.

Let the marmalade cool before pouring into a sterilized Kilner/Mason jar and refrigerating.

TECHNIQUES
TEMPERING CHOCOLATE

Tempering chocolate is essentially the method of melting and cooling chocolate in a specific way so that it has a high shine and wonderful snap when you break it. It is an essential skill for any budding pastry chef and means that you can handle and store chocolate at room temperature, which allows you to manipulate and shape the chocolate in any way you like and create beautiful decorations.

Once you understand the science behind it, it is quite straightforward. All chocolate is made up of six different fats. Four of these are classed as unstable and the other two are stable. Tempering chocolate is the process of trying to emulsify all of the fats together and work with them in the stable fat temperature zone, this allows the chocolate to display all of the characteristics mentioned above (smooth, shiny etc.). All store-bought chocolate is already tempered and melting it causes the fats to separate and if not tempered back can cause the chocolate to 'bloom', which tastes and looks grainy. Different brands of chocolate claim to have slightly different temperatures to temper at, my advice would be to check the packaging. It is best to use chocolate buttons, finely chopped chocolate or callets. However, the range of temperatures listed below should work very well for most brands.

Dark/bittersweet chocolate heat to above 45°C (113°F) then cool to 27°C–31°C (80°F–88°F)
Milk/semisweet chocolate heat to above 40°C (104°F) then cool to 27°C–31°C (80°F–88°F)
White chocolate heat to above 40°C (104°F) then cool to 27°C–31°C (80°F–88°F)

The temperatures listed above should always be adhered to, no matter the method of tempering. The different methods come into play when cooling the chocolate down. There are two main ways of doing this: the marble method and the ice bath

method. For the marble method you need a clean, dry marble work surface or slab, digital thermometer, angled palette knife/metal spatula and pâtisserie scraper. First, melt all the chocolate in short bursts in the microwave or in a bain-marie to the correct temperature (see list, left). Pour four-fifths of it onto the marble surface and use the palette knife/metal spatula to spread it as thinly as possible to allow the chocolate to cool (**A**). Keep it moving and use the scraper to bring the chocolate back into the centre of the work surface (**B**). Using the thermometer, check the temperature of the chocolate and continue spreading and scraping in the same way as it cools and slightly thickens, until the temperature reads 27°C (80°F). Quickly pour the chocolate on the slab back into the one-fifth of chocolate left in the bowl and stir for 1 minute, this should bring the temperature back to around 30°C (86°F). The chocolate is now tempered and ready to start working with (**C**). If it is cooler you can warm it up a little but be careful as you can easily warm too much 33/34°C (92/93°F) and untemper the chocolate.

For the ice bath method, you need a large bowl of ice and a digital thermometer. Gently melt all of the chocolate over a bain-marie to the correct temperature (see left). Put the bowl of chocolate into another larger bowl filled with ice and stir constantly as the chocolate cools. After about 30 seconds, move the bowl back over the hot water. Continue moving the bowl of chocolate back and forth from ice to hot water, constantly stirring and checking the temperature until it reaches 30°C (86°F) and the chocolate is tempered. Take care not to get any water into the chocolate as this will ruin it.

You can then spread the tempered chocolate in a thin layer on a sheet of acetate (**D**). Cut to your desired size while the chocolate is still wet (**E**), then leave to set and carefully remove the acetate (**F**) leaving behind the tempered chocolate decorations.

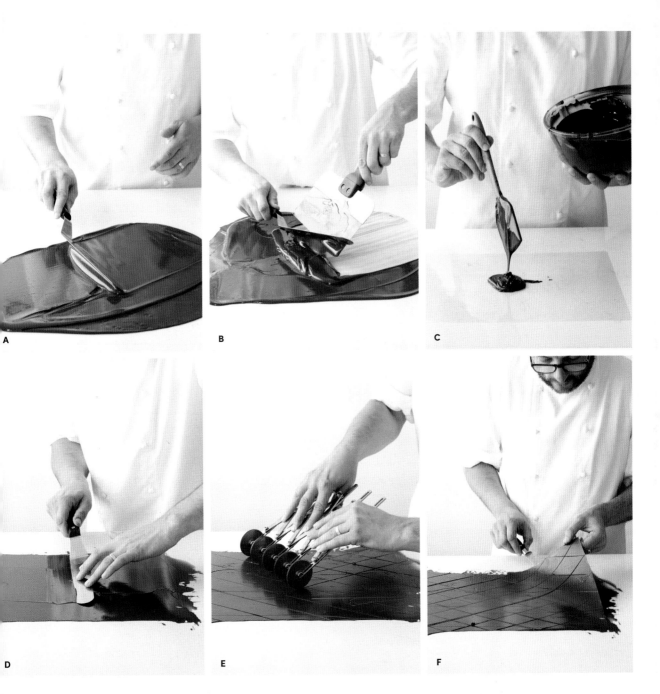

QUENELLING

Quenelling is a technique which has been around since the birth of haute cuisine in the 1970s. It's a way of moulding soft foods such as whipped cream, ice cream, sorbet, ganache or butter into an attractive smooth oval shape. It adds a real professional touch and is the perfect elegant way to serve an accompaniment. You will see that I have used a quenelle in some form or another on quite a few of the desserts throughout this book.

It may look easy enough but it is actually quite a difficult skill to teach because it is really all about practise. If this is something you would like to master, I strongly advise that you buy yourself some double/heavy cream, whip it until very firm and keep trying until you perfect the technique.

There are two different ways you can make a quenelle. The method I first learned in the early 1990s was the traditional two spoon method. This is the way that most chefs learn when they are starting out. To do this, simply take a generous scoop of cream in one spoon, gently press the bowl of the second spoon into the cream and scoop into the second spoon. Smoothly transfer the cream back and forth between the two spoons until it is shaped into a smooth egg with slightly pointed ends; a quenelle.

The method I am using in the images (left) is more commonly known in professional terms as a rocher, because it is made with one spoon rather than two. It still makes the original quenelle shape but is a more contemporary method.

For the rocher or two spoon method, fill a jug/pitcher with hot water and place one or several dessert spoons in there ready. In a perfect world you would use silver spoons, but I appreciate this is not very practical. You can also buy special 'quenelle spoons' which have a deep, round base ideal for moulding the shape. But most people find that a dessert spoon is more than sufficient. You want the water to be just the right temperature: hot enough to help the food to slide off the spoon but not so boiling that it causes the quenelle to melt.

A helpful tip, which is not essential but will help with your practise, is to use a square or rectangular container with high, firm sides. Anything at all will do really but this will give you a straight edge to finish off the quenelle.

Take the dessert spoon out of the hot water, shake off any drips and immediately dig the spoon into the cream sideways to fill it and in one smooth swoop drag it towards the flat side of the container **(A)**. The idea is to do this in a smooth dig and swoop motion. The cream should begin to curl round as you go. Press against the side of the container to scoop out and lift up the cream, if you are not immediately happy with the shape then go back into the container and push the quenelle against the cream in the tub to spin it round in the hot spoon and smooth the edges.

Once you have the shape you require, rub the bottom of the spoon on the palm of your hand **(B)** (don't worry, you won't come into contact with the food and you of course will place the spoon back into the water before you quenelle again) this will help create a little friction and heat and will make removing the quenelle from the spoon easier **(C)**.

The more you practise these techniques, the better you will be. It is worth all the effort and tremendously satisfying when you achieve a perfect smooth round quenelle or rocher.

You can make smaller dainty little quenelles using a teaspoon, too **(D)**.

SPHERIFICATION

This is a modern technique that produces stunning contemporary garnishes or even integral elements to add to desserts such as my Hot Sake Jelly Shots (see page 148). It was pioneered by renowned Spanish chef Ferran Adria and essentially it is the culinary process of shaping flavoured liquid into perfect spheres by submerging it in a solution. The spheres not only look beautiful but burst with flavour in a delightful way when eaten.

There are fundamentally two main ways of achieving spherification: forward and reverse. The forward method is a lot more user-friendly and it will add a fantastic bit of theatre to your dinner party so that is what I have demonstrated in the images (opposite). I used to teach the forward method years ago and students loved it, because it is very easy to prepare and produces amazing results. I will try to cut through the jargon and explain things in a simple way but once you have the kit you need, it is actually a fairly straightforward process.

THINGS YOU WILL NEED

Spherification is a natural chemical reaction between sodium alginate (from the cell walls of brown seaweed) and calcium chloride (essentially from limestone). You can buy these as part of a spherification kit from some of the companies listed in my suppliers list (see page 176). These kits will also include tools such as a spherification spoon, pipette for dropping the solution, litmus paper for testing the PH and a PH guide – if you don't buy a kit you will have to purchase these things separately. You will also need some white sugar. I find that using a hand blender at the start of the process is the best way to combine the sodium alginate into the liquid to disperse it evenly, so it really helps if you have one of these. A small fine-mesh sieve/strainer is also useful for washing the spherification once made.

NOW FOR THE SCIENCEY BIT!

You can use pretty much any flavourful liquid that you like for this technique, so long as it is not lactic and it fits within the required PH scale. What you are trying to achieve is a solution of flavourful liquid and sodium alginate that is between 2 and 8 on the PH scale. Once you have this you can drop it into a water bath solution that contains calcium chloride and this will cause a reaction that sets the sodium alginate.

There are several ways that you can adjust the PH ratio required. If you are making a spherification with sake or alcohol for example, these tend to be quite high on the PH scale, around 7 or 8. So adding a little cold sugar syrup (2 parts water to 1 part sugar boiled until the sugar has dissolved) will help to neutralize and bring the PH back towards the middle, thus making a better gelling liquid.

STEP-BY-STEP

First, use a hand blender to blend the sodium alginate and sugar into half of the flavourful liquid you want to spherify (A). Note, in my recipe on page 148 this is the ginger syrup. Blending only half the liquid to start with means that you won't add too much air into the mixture, thus making better spheres. Next, stir in the remaining flavourful liquid (B). Carefully use a pipette or cook's squeeze bottle to drop individual droplets of the liquid into a water bath that has the desired amount of calcium chloride (C). The best height from which to let the drops fall will vary according to the texture of the liquid you are using, so you may need to experiment until you get it just right. Leave for about 30 seconds for the membrane to form around the liquid. Finally, rinse the spherification with clean water over a fine-mesh sieve/strainer before serving immediately (D).

A

B

C

D

FINISHING TOUCHES

There is an old saying that I'm sure we are all familiar with which is, you eat with your eyes first. This is especially important when you are making quite difficult and elaborate recipes, like some included in this book. There is nothing worse than putting incredible amounts of time and effort into your creation, only for you to feel disappointed in how it looks when you present this to your guests. A high finish is obviously easier to achieve when you are a professionally trained pastry chef, but if I'm honest, that is only really because you have practised and failed enough times to work out your own style. Practise and an understanding of how you want your creation to look once you have finished are the two most important things of any of the techniques outlined in this book. Having that final goal in sight will really help you work towards the finished article. I would suggest in general that you start with some of the simpler recipes in this book so that you don't stretch yourself too early. Using simple decorative finishes effectively will make you more confident to try new things and therefore increase your skill and understanding. There are many little tips and tricks that will elevate your desserts, I have listed the uses and usage occasions below.

LUSTRE POWDERS & SILVER & GOLD LEAF: these can both add a really stylish finishing touch. My advice here is to use these sparingly and in the right application, a little flash of shimmer can really elevate the clean lines of your creations but too much can look quite garish so use small amounts in a tasteful manner. Use tweezers to apply the foils and a small food safe paint brush or tea strainer to apply the lustre powders.

FROSTING/DUSTING: this is a really good way of introducing softness and colour to your finished desserts. A fine sprinkling of bright green matcha powder or simple icing/confectioners' sugar will lift any surface, whether dark/bittersweet chocolate or a light pastry. Just remember what you are dusting onto and when you need to serve, things like icing/confectioners' sugar will disappear very quickly, so a good little tip is to mix the sugar with a little bit of cornflour/cornstarch, which helps it to stay on for longer. The best advice really though is to apply a light dusting just before you are about to serve.

PIPING: these days piping is a far more accessible craft than it has ever been, from specialist shops to general stores you can pretty much pick up everything you need to facilitate some fine piping. The key things to remember are as follows:

- Use the right nozzle/tip – so many times piping can look clumsy because the nozzle is either too small or too large in scale to the dessert you are working on.
- Never fill the piping/pastry bag any further than half-full. This will allow you to have control over your piping, you can always add more into the bag if you need it.
- Practise, practise, practise before you undertake any piping onto your finished dessert, have a practise on a piece of baking parchment first, this will allow you to get that all-important confidence in how quickly the filling will come out and how large or small the line you are drawing will be.

SMALL CAKES & INDIVIDUAL PÂTISSERIE

THIS CHAPTER INCLUDES A SELECTION OF INDIVIDUALLY PORTIONED TRADITIONAL PÂTISSERIE ITEMS, EACH WITH A LITTLE TWIST, AS WELL AS A COUPLE OF TRULY UNIQUE AND MODERN CREATIONS. FROM PARIS-BREST TO KOUIGN-AMANN, ÉCLAIRS AND SCONES, THESE TREATS ARE PERFECT TO SERVE ON THEIR OWN, OR AS PART OF AN AFTERNOON TEA.

MATCHA, PINK PEPPERCORN & WILD STRAWBERRY MADELEINES

These buttery scalloped French sponges are best baked just before serving. The addition of matcha powder turns them a brilliant shade of green and superbly complements the sweetness. If wild strawberries are not available, they can be substituted with small berries of your choice such as blueberries or raspberries.

150 g/1¼ sticks butter, diced
50 g/½ cup ground almonds
¾ tablespoon matcha
   powder
50 g/generous ⅓ cup plain/
   all-purpose flour
150 g/5¼ oz. egg whites
150 g/¾ cup caster/
   granulated sugar
½ tablespoon pink
   peppercorns, ground
24 wild strawberries, hulled
   and rinsed
strawberry jam/jelly or curd,
   to serve (optional)

12–hole scalloped madeleine
   mould or pan, greased well
   with oil spray
piping/pastry bag with a large
   plain nozzle/tip (optional)

MAKES 12 MADELEINES

First, make a beurre noisette (browned butter). Put the diced butter in a saucepan and set over medium-high heat for around 5–7 minutes until melted and boiling. The fat at the bottom of the pan should start to go a nutty-brown colour, but be careful this does not darken too much and burn. Transfer the browned butter immediately to a heatproof dish and set aside to cool until just warm.

In a separate bowl, sift together the ground almonds, matcha powder and flour. In another separate bowl, whisk together the egg whites with the sugar until frothy. Carefully fold the dry ingredients, warm beurre noisette and ground pink peppercorns into the sugar and egg mixture until fully incorporated and no lumps remain. Transfer the mixture to the fridge to chill for a minimum of 1 hour.

Preheat the oven to 180°C (350°F) Gas 4.

Put the chilled madeleine mixture into the piping/pastry bag and pipe in enough to fill the greased moulds. Alternatively, you can spoon the mixture in. Press two wild strawberries into the centre of each madeleine and bake in the preheated oven for 10–12 minutes until risen and golden-green.

Remove the madeleine pan or mould from the oven and allow to stand for a minute. Remove the cakes from their moulds and serve warm with strawberry jam/jelly or curd on the side, if desired.

MONT BLANC

This traditional French patisserie item is a favourite in Japan, probably due to the popularity of chestnuts in that part of the world. It gets its name because of the resemblance to a snow-capped mountain. I have used a traditional sablé Breton (French butter cookie) recipe for the base, which adds a real touch of indulgence.

SABLÉ BRETON BASE
3 egg yolks
80 g/scant ½ cup maple sugar (or use Demerara/turbinado sugar if not available)
80 g/¾ stick butter
110 g/¾ cup plus 1½ tablespoons plain/all-purpose flour
¾ tablespoon baking powder

MONT BLANC FILLING
100 g/scant ½ cup whipping/heavy cream
100 g/scant ½ cup mascarpone cheese
seeds from 2 vanilla pods/beans
100 g/scant ¾ cup icing/confectioners' sugar

CHESTNUT PASTE
200 g/¾ cup sweet chestnut cream
200 g/¾ cup chestnut purée
3½ tablespoons dark rum

TO DECORATE
marrons glacés (candied chestnuts)
gold leaf (optional)
icing/confectioners' sugar

stand mixer with whisk and paddle attachments
6 individual 8-cm/3-inch tart pans
6 demi-sphere moulds
piping/pastry bags with a plain nozzle/tip and a Mont Blanc/grass nozzle/tip

MAKES 6 MONT BLANC

Preheat the oven to 160°C (325°F) Gas 3.

To make the sablé Breton base, put the egg yolks and maple sugar in the bowl of a stand mixer with a whisk attachment and beat together until light and fluffy. Change to the paddle attachment and beat in the butter followed by the flour and baking powder until well incorporated and the mixture comes together to form a smooth dough.

Press the dough straight into the six individual tart pans using your fingers, making sure that there are no gaps and the thickness is even. Bake the sablé Breton in the preheated oven for around 10–12 minutes until golden brown. Remove from the oven and let cool in the pans before turning out and setting aside until needed.

To make the Mont Blanc filling, beat all the ingredients together using a balloon whisk until semi-whipped. Transfer to the piping/pastry bag with the plain nozzle/tip and pipe into the six demi-sphere moulds to fill. Scrape level and freeze the fillings for around 2 hours or until completely frozen solid.

To make the chestnut paste, mix all the ingredients together until well combined and transfer to the piping/pastry bag fitted with the Mont Blanc/grass nozzle/tip. Set aside ready for constructing the desserts.

To construct the desserts, arrange the sablé Breton bases on serving plates and remove the frozen Mont Blanc fillings from their demi-sphere moulds. Put a Mont Blanc filling on each of the sablé Breton bases.

Starting at the base of the dessert, pipe the chestnut paste around the Mont Blanc in a circular motion, winding up and around to gradually cover all the filling and finish in a point at the top. Repeat for each dessert. Crown the desserts with marrons glacés (candied chestnuts), add a little gold leaf if you like and finally dust with icing/confectioners' sugar to finish.

TONKA BEAN, MILK CHOCOLATE & RASPBERRY DESSERTS

This is a rework of the framboisier dessert we made for The Great British Bake off: Crème de la Crème *with a coconut joconde sponge base, raspberry and blood orange jelly and silky chocolate mousse. A homage to the exceptional Graham Mairs.*

BLOOD ORANGE & RASPBERRY JELLY

25 g/1¾ tablespoons caster/ granulated sugar

160 g/5½ oz. seedless raspberry purée (I use the Boiron brand)

1½ large sheets or 3 small domestic leaves of gelatine, soaked in cold water

2¾ tablespoons blood orange juice

CHEESECAKE CREAM

150 ml/⅔ cup whipping/ heavy cream

500 g/2 cups mascarpone cheese

seeds from 1 Tahitian vanilla pod/bean

2 large sheets or 4 small domestic leaves of gelatine, dissolved in 1 tablespoon warm water

60 g/3 tablespoons trimoline inverted sugar

COCONUT JOCONDE SPONGE

185 g/2⅓ cups desiccated/ dried shredded coconut

185 g/scant 1⅓ cups icing/ confectioners' sugar

5 eggs

50 g/generous ⅓ cup plain/ all-purpose flour

5 egg whites

25 g/1¾ tablespoons caster/ granulated sugar

45 g/3¼ tablespoons butter, melted

continued overleaf

To make the blood orange and raspberry jelly, combine the sugar with one-third of the raspberry purée in a saucepan over medium-high heat. Put a sugar thermometer in the pan and bring the mixture to boiling point. Once boiling, add the remaining raspberry purée and heat until the mixture reaches 90°C (194°F). Remove from the heat, then squeeze out the soaked gelatine leaves and mix in along with the blood orange juice. Allow the jelly to cool slightly before pouring into four of the insert moulds to fill halfway up. Transfer to the fridge for 1–2 hours until set.

To make the cheesecake cream, set aside 3½ tablespoons of the whipping/heavy cream and semi-whip the rest. In a clean bowl, mix the mascarpone with the vanilla seeds, dissolved gelatine, 3½ tablespoons of unwhipped whipping/heavy cream and the trimoline inverted sugar. Fold in the semi-whipped cream, then pour into the insert moulds on top of the set jelly and transfer to the freezer to set; 1–2 hours.

To make the coconut joconde sponge that will act as the base of the desserts, put the desiccated/dried shredded coconut, icing/confectioners' sugar and whole eggs in a mixing bowl and beat together using a hand-held electric whisk until light and fluffy. Beat in the flour until combined. Set aside.

Preheat the oven to 210°C (410°F) Gas 6.

Put the egg whites in a separate bowl and whisk using a hand-held electric whisk until soft peaks form. Increase the speed of the mixer and slowly add the sugar to make a stiff and glossy meringue mixture. Carefully fold the meringue into the egg and flour mixture trying not to knock out the air. Fold in the melted butter. Spread the cake batter in an even layer onto the prepared baking sheet. Bake in the preheated oven for around 8 minutes or until a little risen and just cooked. Remove from the oven and then turn the baking sheet upside down onto another sheet of baking parchment and peel off the paper on the back.

To make the chocolate and tonka bean mousse, put the double/heavy cream and tonka essence in a saucepan over medium heat and bring just to the boil. Remove from the heat and pour over the milk/semisweet chocolate. Leave to stand for a minute until the heat from the cream has melted the chocolate, then stir into a smooth ganache. Cool a little, then fold in the semi-whipped whipping/heavy cream. Transfer to the piping/pastry bag and put in the fridge until needed.

A

B

C

D

CHOCOLATE & TONKA BEAN MOUSSE

500 ml/generous 2 cups double/heavy cream

1 teaspoon tonka bean essence or freshly grated tonka beans

1 kg/2¼ lb. milk/semisweet chocolate

500 ml/generous 2 cups whipping/heavy cream, semi-whipped

RASPBERRY ESPUMA SPONGE GARNISH (OPTIONAL)

80 g/generous ⅓ cup caster/granulated sugar

210 g/1½ cups cake flour (or plain/all-purpose flour if not available)

240 g/8½ oz. egg whites

60 g/⅔ cup raspberry powder (available online)

50 g/generous ⅓ cup icing/confectioners' sugar

RED CHOCOLATE SPRAY

store-bought red chocolate velvet aerosol spray (see suppliers page 176)
OR if you have a patisserie food-grade spray gun:

300 g/10½ oz. white chocolate

200 g/7 oz. cocoa butter

approx. 50 g/1¾ oz. red cocoa butter colouring

shards of tempered chocolate, to decorate

sugar thermometer
4 large moulds, plus 4 insert moulds that will fit inside
baking sheet, lined with non-stick baking parchment
piping/pastry bag with a plain nozzle/tip
espuma gun and polystyrene cup, for the micro sponge (optional)

MAKES 4 DESSERTS

To make the raspberry espuma sponge garnish (if using), mix all the ingredients together, fill into a syphon or espuma gun and gas twice. Squeeze into a polystyrene cup and microwave for 40 seconds. Remove from the microwave, cut into pieces and set aside for plating.

To construct the desserts, remove the raspberry jelly and cheesecake cream inserts from their moulds, wrap in clingfilm/plastic wrap and then return these to the freezer until required. Make sure you have all the components and equipment to hand. Position the large mould on top of the joconde sponge and cut out four pieces of sponge to form the bases for the desserts. Set aside for a moment.

Pipe a small amount of chocolate mousse into the large moulds and use a small palette knife/metal spatula to spread around the walls to ensure all the surfaces are covered **(A)**. Pipe in more chocolate mousse, filling about two-thirds of the way up and ensuring every single nook and cranny is filled. Tap down on the work surface to get rid of any air bubbles.

Position the frozen cheesecake and jelly layer in the centre of each mould **(B)**. Push down gently to make sure they are fully inserted. Pipe around these layers with more chocolate mousse and again gently tap the mould on the work surface to knock out any remaining air bubbles. Set the pieces of cut-out joconde sponge on top **(C)**, pressing down gently before returning to the freezer to set; 1–2 hours.

When completely set, carefully remove the desserts from their moulds and transfer to a sheet of non-stick baking parchment to protect the work surface. If you have a professional spray gun, melt the white chocolate, cocoa butter and red colouring separately in either a microwave or over a bain-marie. Mix the melted chocolate and the cocoa butter together, then stir in the red colouring. Transfer to the spray gun to use immediately, or use store-bought velvet aerosol spray, to spray the desserts red all over **(D)**.

Garnish the finished desserts with a small dot of melted chocolate to stick on the espuma sponge (if using) and shards of tempered chocolate in the style of your choosing.

MATCHA CHOUX BUNS WITH CRAQUELIN TOPPING & VANILLA CUSTARD

Everyone will love this treat with its simple, clean and sweet flavours. Craquelin (also known as suikerbrood, or sugar bread) is a wickedly delicious sugary dough topping. As the choux buns bake, the topping expands and cracks to give a wonderful crunchy layer. The tempered white chocolate ring surrounding these buns is optional but it does look stunning. The component parts can be made separately in advance.

CRAQUELIN TOPPING
50 g/3½ tablespoons butter, softened
50 g/¼ cup light brown soft sugar
50 g/generous ⅓ cup plain/all-purpose flour
25 g/¼ cup ground almonds
¾ teaspoon sea salt
30 g/5 level tablespoons matcha powder

CHOUX BUNS
½ quantity Choux Pastry (see page 12)
matcha powder, to dust

VANILLA CRÈME DIPLOMAT FILLING
1 quantity Crème Diplomat (see page 16)

MATCHA FONDANT
300 g/2 cups plus 2 tablespoons fondant icing/confectioners' sugar
20 g/3½ tablespoons matcha powder

To make the craquelin topping, combine all the ingredients together in a mixing bowl and mix with a wooden spoon to form a smooth paste. Roll out the paste between two sheets of non-stick baking parchment until about 2 mm/¹⁄₁₀ inch thick. Freeze the dough between the baking parchment sheets for around 20 minutes or until firm enough to cut. Once firm enough, stamp out 16 discs using the 5-cm/2-inch cookie cutter. Wrap the discs in clingfilm/plastic wrap and return to the freezer until needed.

Preheat the oven to 170°C (350°F) Gas 4.

To make the choux buns, prepare the Choux Pastry following the instructions on page 12. Once the pastry has reached dropping consistency, transfer to a piping/pastry bag. Use a stencil to help if you wish, and pipe 16 small neat round balls spaced well apart onto the lined baking sheet. They should be no bigger than 4 cm/1½ inches in diameter as they will rise and need to be small enough to fit inside their chocolate ring.

Top the raw choux pastry balls with a disc each of frozen craquelin and bake in the preheated oven for around 20 minutes until risen and golden or until a perfect crust has formed all the way around the choux when cut in half. Transfer to a wire rack to cool.

To make the Vanilla Crème Diplomat filling, prepare the Crème Diplomat following the instructions on page 16. Scrape into a piping/pastry bag and refrigerate until required.

To make the matcha fondant, mix together the fondant icing/confectioners' sugar and matcha powder with around 1 tablespoon of water or enough to give a thick yet pipeable consistency. Transfer to a piping/pastry bag and set aside until required.

continued overleaf

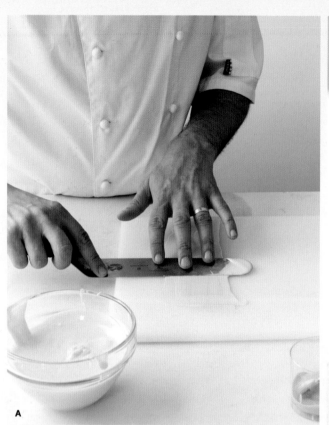

TEMPERED CHOCOLATE RING (OPTIONAL)

green cocoa butter colouring
approx. 300 g/10½ oz.
 tempered white chocolate
 (see method on page 20)

*5-cm/2-inch round cookie
 cutter*
*3 piping/pastry bags with
 plain nozzles/tips*
*baking sheet, lined with
 non-stick baking parchment*
acetate roll
6-cm/3-inch cake rings
*electric temperature probe,
 for tempering the chocolate*

MAKES 8 DESSERTS
(16 CHOUX BUNS)

To make the white chocolate rings (if using), make sure you have all the equipment to hand as the chocolate will set quickly once tempered. Cut the acetate into 10 strips about 15 cm/6 inches long (you only need to make 8 rings in total but a couple of spares are useful). Set aside ready to use.

Temper the chocolate following the instructions on page 20. Set aside about 50 g/1¾ oz. of the tempered chocolate and add a few drops of green cocoa butter colouring to the rest and mix until you are happy with the colour. Using a pastry brush, apply long straight lines of green-coloured chocolate to the length of each strip of acetate on the inside of the natural curve. Leave aside to dry for a few minutes.

Once completely dry, use a palette knife/metal spatula to smear a generous amount of tempered white chocolate on top of the green colouring in an even layer – do no more than two of these at a time as this is quite a tricky process (**A**). Leave for a moment until the chocolate layer is just starting to set, then fold round to make a circle with the chocolate on the inside (**B**). Push the open end into the still slightly sticky chocolate to try and create a neat seam. Slot the chocolate-covered acetate into a metal cake ring and leave to set (**C**). Repeat with the rest of the chocolate and acetate until you have the eight, leave them all to set and then refrigerate until needed.

To construct the desserts, make a small hole in the bottom of the choux buns and pipe in a generous amount of vanilla crème diplomat filling to each. Remove the chocolate-covered acetate from the metal cake rings but leave the acetate on the chocolate for the moment.

 Dust the buns with matcha powder. Gently insert one bun into the side of a white chocolate ring and pipe some matcha fondant into the other end. Press in another choux bun on top of the fondant to sandwich the two together (**D**) at either end of the ring. The matcha fondant will be the glue to hold the components together.

Now carefully remove the acetate from around the outside of the white chocolate ring – do not do this before filling the ring because it acts as a support for the chocolate. Refrigerate for 1 hour until everything has set and the desserts are ready to serve.

LEMON & YUZU ÉCLAIRS

The sharp, fragrant tang of yuzu juice is a surprising yet delicious addition to the classic French éclair. This recipe is worth a little effort as the results are stunning.

½ quantity Choux Pastry
   (see page 12)
1 beaten egg yolk, to glaze

YUZU & LEMON CREAM
300 ml/1¼ cups yuzu juice
a small squeeze of fresh
   lemon juice, to taste
seeds from 1 vanilla pod/bean
4 egg yolks
25 g/¼ cup cornflour/
   cornstarch
75 g/⅓ cup plus 2 teaspoons
   caster/superfine sugar
a pinch of salt
30 g/¼ stick butter, softened
100 ml/scant ½ cup double/
   heavy cream

**WHITE CHOCOLATE & YUZU
FONDANT**
200 ml/generous ¾ cup
   yuzu juice
juice of ½ lemon
80 g/½ cup minus
   1 tablespoon caster/
   superfine sugar
50 g/1¾ oz. white chocolate,
   chopped
200 g/7 oz. store-bought
   fondant, warmed
a few drops of yellow food
   colouring (optional)
melted white chocolate,
   chocolate discs and silver
   leaf, to decorate (optional)

*2 piping/pastry bags with a
   large-star shaped nozzle/tip
   and a small plain nozzle/tip
baking sheet, lined with
   non-stick baking parchment*

MAKES 8 ÉCLAIRS

Prepare the Choux Pastry following the method on page 12. Once the pastry has reached dropping consistency transfer to the piping/pastry bag fitted with a large star-shaped nozzle/tip.

Preheat the oven to 200°C (400°F) Gas 6.

Pipe eight 12 cm/4½-inch long straight lines onto the prepared baking sheet. Space them evenly apart and use a stencil to guide you if needed. Hold the bag at an angle and be careful not to pipe the choux too flat as this could stop it from rising properly. Brush the dough with the beaten egg yolk and bake in the preheated oven for around 10–15 minutes or until risen, golden and cooked through. Leave to cool on a wire rack.

To make the yuzu and lemon cream, heat the yuzu juice, lemon juice and seeds from the vanilla pod/bean together in a small saucepan until just boiling. In a clean mixing bowl, whisk together the egg yolks, cornflour/cornstarch, sugar and salt. Carefully and slowly pour the boiling yuzu mixture into the dry ingredients, whisking until the dry ingredients are fully incorporated. Pour everything back into the pan and return to medium heat. Whisk constantly for 2–3 minutes to cook out the cornflour/cornstarch. Transfer the mixture to a bowl and whisk occasionally while letting cool. When the mixture has cooled a little, beat in the softened butter. Once completely cool, whisk in the double/heavy cream until fully incorporated. Transfer the yuzu and lemon cream to the clean piping/pastry bag with a plain nozzle/tip and chill in the refrigerator until needed.

To make the white chocolate and yuzu fondant, put the yuzu juice, lemon juice and sugar in a small saucepan and boil for 15–20 minutes until the mixture has reduced by half into a syrup. Set aside to cool a little. Meanwhile, melt the white chocolate in a heatproof bowl set over a pan of barely simmering water. Make sure the base of the bowl does not touch the water. Stir the melted chocolate into the warmed store-bought fondant. Add the cooled yuzu syrup to taste and stir in a few drops of yellow food colouring (if needed) to give a stronger (but still delicate) yellow colour.

To construct the éclairs, make two small holes in the base at either end of the cooled choux, then gently pipe the chilled yuzu and lemon cream inside from either end to meet in the middle. Dip one long side of each éclair in the white chocolate and yuzu fondant, wiping away any untidy edges. Put the iced éclairs in the fridge to chill for 5 minutes.

To decorate, pipe a fine line of melted white chocolate diagonally end to end. Add a white chocolate disc and some silver leaf, if desired.

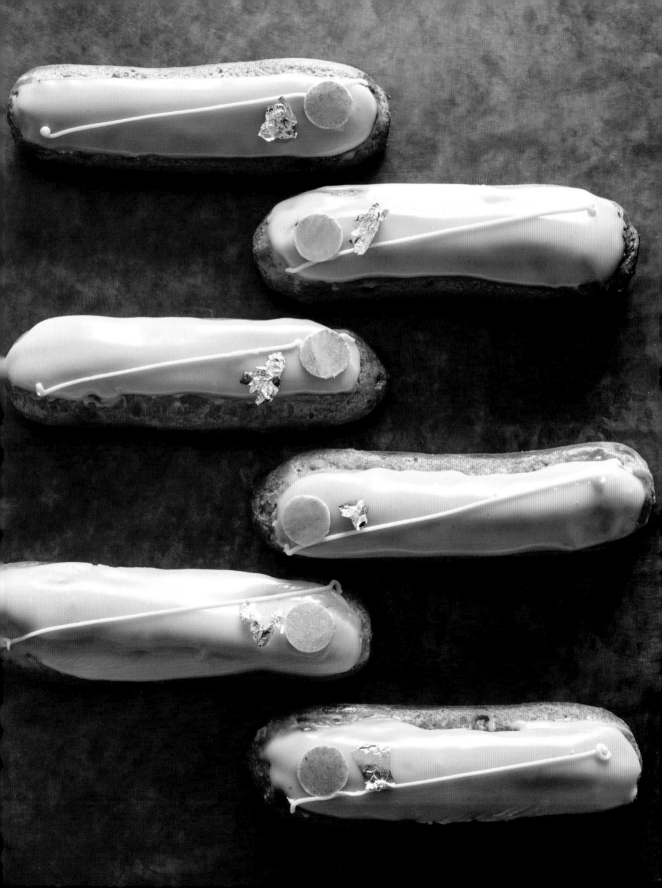

PARIS-BREST WITH HAZELNUT PRALINE & KOSHIAN MOUSSE

I have given this legendary French pastry dessert a Japanese twist with the addition of koshian (a sweetened adzuki bean paste) to the mousse filling. You can choose to make the koshian paste yourself using my recipe (see page 19), or you can purchase it ready-made online quite easily. Combined with a classic hazelnut praline mousse, the finished dessert is rather beautiful and perfect for sharing.

VANILLA CRUNCH TOPPING

50 g/3½ tablespoons butter, softened

50 g/¼ cup light brown soft sugar

50 g/generous ⅓ cup plain/all-purpose flour

25 g/¼ cup ground almonds

¾ teaspoon sea salt

seeds from ¼ vanilla pod/bean

CHOUX RINGS

½ quantity Choux Pastry (see page 12)

HAZELNUT PRALINE MOUSSE & KOSHIAN MOUSSE

70 ml/scant ⅓ cup milk

60 g/¼ cup caster/superfine sugar

1 teaspoon vanilla extract

3 large sheets or 6 small domestic leaves of gelatine, soaked in cold water

65 g/scant ¼ cup hazelnut praline paste

120 g/⅔ cup koshian paste (store-bought or see my recipe page 19)

520 g/2¼ cups mascarpone cheese

560 ml/2½ cups whipping/heavy cream

PRALINE DECORATION

100 g/1¼ cups flaked/slivered almonds

200 g/1½ cups minus 1 tablespoon icing/confectioners' sugar, plus extra for dusting

7.5-cm/3-inch round cookie cutters and 5.5-cm/2-inch round cookie cutters

3 piping/pastry bags with a large plain nozzle/tip and 2 star-shaped nozzles/tips

2 baking sheets, lined with non-stick baking parchment

MAKES 8 PASTRIES

To make the vanilla crunch topping, combine all the ingredients and stir together to form a smooth, thick paste. Roll out the paste until around 2 mm/¹⁄₁₀ inch thick between two sheets of non-stick baking parchment. Freeze between the paper for around 30 minutes or until set and firm enough to cut. Stamp out eight circles using the larger round cookie cutter, then cut another eight circles out of the middle of each using the smaller round cookie cutter to create eight rings (discarding the offcuts from the middle). Wrap the rings in clingfilm/plastic wrap and freeze until firm.

Preheat the oven to 200°C (400°F) Gas 6.

To make the choux rings, prepare the Choux Pastry following the method on page 12. Once the pastry has reached dropping consistency transfer to a piping/pastry bag with the large star-shaped nozzle/tip. Pipe eight 7.5-cm/3-inch rings of choux pastry, four on each of the two prepared baking sheets, using a stencil to guide you if needed. Lay a frozen ring of vanilla crunch on top of each choux ring. Bake the choux in the preheated oven for around 10–15 minutes or until the pastry is risen, golden and cooked through. Remove the baking sheet from the oven and leave on a wire rack to cool.

To make the hazelnut praline mousse and the koshian mousse, combine the milk, sugar and vanilla extract in a small saucepan and bring just to the boil over medium heat. Remove from the heat, then squeeze out the soaked gelatine and stir in. Separate the mixture into two equal halves and add the hazelnut praline paste to one and the koshian paste to the other. Stir to combine fully and allow both mixtures to cool to room temperature. Whisk half the mascarpone cheese and half the whipping/heavy cream into each until lightly whipped. Scrape both into two separate piping/pastry bags fitted with star-shaped nozzles/tips and chill in the refrigerator until needed.

To make the praline decoration, toss the flaked/slivered almonds with the icing/confectioners' sugar. Toast in a dry frying pan/skillet until golden. Add a splash of water and heat until caramelized. Pour onto a sheet of non-stick baking parchment and leave to set firm before breaking up into large clusters.

To construct the desserts, cut each of the choux rings in half horizontally. On the base of each pipe five rosettes of hazelnut mousse leaving enough space to pipe another five rosettes of koshian mousse inbetween. Once the choux ring is filled with alternate rosettes of both mousses, put the lid gently on top and dust lightly with icing/confectioners' sugar. Pipe three more rosettes of mousse on top and add three clusters of praline decoration.

CRUNCHY CARAMELIZED CUSTARD BUNS WITH MATCHA & VANILLA

The inspiration for this simple yet delicious pastry came from a research trip to Tokyo's famous Custard Lab. I loved their version so much that I had to come up with my own.

CHOUX BUNS
½ quantity Choux Pastry
 (see page 12)
2 beaten egg yolks, to glaze

MATCHA CUSTARD
300 ml/1¼ cups whole milk
seeds from 1 Tahitian vanilla
 pod/bean
4 egg yolks
25 g/¼ cup cornflour/
 cornstarch
1 tablespoon matcha powder
75 g/generous ⅓ cup caster/
 superfine sugar
a pinch of salt
30 g/¼ stick butter, softened
100 ml/scant ½ cup double/
 heavy cream

PALMIERS
200 g/7 oz. store-bought
 puff pastry
icing/confectioners' sugar,
 for dusting

2 piping/pastry bags with
 a large plain nozzle/tip
 and small plain nozzle/tip
2 baking sheets, lined with
 non-stick baking parchment
heavy baking tray

MAKES 8 BUNS

Preheat the oven to 200°C (400°F) Gas 6.

To make the choux buns, prepare the Choux Pastry following the method on page 12. Once the pastry has reached dropping consistency transfer to the piping/pastry bag fitted with the large plain nozzle/tip. Pipe eight balls spaced spaced evenly apart onto one of the prepared baking sheet in 6-cm/2½-inch rounds, using a stencil to guide you if needed. Brush with beaten egg yolks and bake in the preheated oven for 10–15 minutes or until risen and golden. Remove from the oven and leave to cool.

To make the matcha custard, put the milk and vanilla seeds in a saucepan and bring to the boil over medium heat. In a separate bowl whisk together the egg yolks, cornflour/cornstarch, matcha powder, sugar and salt. Pour over the hot milk and whisk until thickened and the dry ingredients have been fully absorbed. Pour everything back into the pan and return to medium heat. Whisk constantly for 2–3 minutes to cook out the cornflour/cornstarch. Transfer to a bowl and whisk occasionally as the mixture cools. After a couple of minutes beat in the softened butter. Once completely cool whisk in the double/heavy cream. Transfer the matcha custard to the piping/pastry bag with the small plain nozzle/tip and refrigerate until needed.

To make the palmiers, very thinly roll out the puff pastry on a worktop lightly dusted with icing/confectioners' sugar. Trim away the edges to make a perfect square. Dust another layer of icing/confectioners' sugar over the pastry and roll it up like a Swiss roll/jelly roll until the size of the spiral is roughly the same as the base of the choux buns. Trim away the untidy ends and rest in the fridge for 20–30 minutes. Use a sharp knife to slice the roll into thin circles around 2 mm/1⁄10 inch thick. Refrigerate for 20 minutes.

Preheat the oven to 200°C (400°F) Gas 6.

Space the palmiers out on the other prepared baking sheet, you may have more than the eight you need for the buns but this doesn't matter.

Put another sheet of baking parchment on top and then rest the heavy baking tray on top – this will stop the pastry from rising too much. Bake in the preheated oven for 15–20 minutes until golden brown. Remove the heavy baking tray and paper and transfer the palmiers to a wire rack to cool.

To construct the pastries, poke a small hole in the base of a choux bun and pipe in a very generous portion of the matcha custard filling. Pipe a large dot of custard on the base of a palmier and stick onto the choux bun where the opening is. Repeat with the rest of the batch of buns and serve.

APRICOT, TAHINI & SESAME DOUGHNUTS

There is something about the combination of warm, rich apricot mixed with nutty savoury notes from tahini and sesame that makes these doughnuts taste sublime.

DOUGHNUTS
30 g/1 oz. fresh yeast or
    15 g/2½ teaspoons instant
    dried yeast
450 g/scant 3¼ cups white/
    strong bread flour
1 teaspoon salt
45 g/scant ¼ cup caster/
    granulated sugar
30 g/1 oz. lightly beaten egg
200 ml/generous ¾ cup
    warm water
45 g/3¼ tablespoons butter,
    melted
vegetable oil, for deep-frying

APRICOT & TAHINI CURD
150 ml/⅔ cup apricot juice
    or purée
4 egg yolks
2 eggs
100 g/½ cup caster/
    granulated sugar
100 g/1 stick minus
    1 tablespoon butter, diced
50 ml/¼ cup tahini
a small squeeze of fresh
    lemon juice, to taste

BLACK SESAME SUGAR
2 tablespoons ground black
    sesame seeds mixed with
    200 g/1 cup caster/
    granulated sugar

stand mixer with a dough hook
10 squares of non-stick baking
    parchment (8 x 8 cm/
    3 x 3 inches), greased
deep-fryer or large heavy-based
    pan suitable for deep-frying
piping/pastry bag with
    a small plain nozzle/tip

MAKES 10 DOUGHNUTS

To make the doughnuts, if using fresh yeast, dissolve the yeast in around 3½ tablespoons warm water (taken from the 200 ml/generous ¾ cup water added later). Leave to dissolve for 15 minutes until frothy. Meanwhile, combine the flour, salt and sugar in the bowl of a stand mixer fitted with a dough hook. If using instant dried yeast, add this to the bowl now. Add the egg and warm water along with the frothy yeast if using. Knead to bring the dough together, adding a little more water if required. Add the melted butter and continue to knead for 10 minutes or until the dough is smooth and elastic. It should feel sticky but not so much that it sticks to your hands. Put the dough in a lightly oiled bowl and cover with clingfilm/plastic wrap. Leave in a warm place for 1 hour to rise.

Divide the dough into ten portions of around 40 g/1½ oz. each and shape into round balls. Put each ball of dough on a greased square of baking parchment and arrange on a tray. Cover loosely with clingfilm/plastic wrap and leave in a warm place to rise for 45–60 minutes, or until doubled in size.

To make the apricot and tahini curd, combine the apricot juice or purée, egg yolks, whole eggs and sugar in a heatproof bowl. Whisk together and set the bowl over a pan of barely simmering water, ensuring that the base of the bowl does not touch the water. Whisk over medium heat for about 5 minutes or until the mixture starts to thicken. Remove from the heat and whisk for 1 minute more, then mix in the diced butter. Allow to cool slightly, then cover with clingfilm/plastic wrap and refrigerate.

When the dough has risen, preheat the oil in a deep-fryer to 180°C (350°F) or half-fill a large pan with vegetable oil and heat until a cube of bread sizzles and rises to the surface instantly. Carefully slide the doughnuts, still on the baking parchment, into the hot oil – the paper will float to the surface and can then be removed. You will probably need to fry in batches of three or four depending on the size of your pan. Cook for around 3 minutes and use a slotted spoon to turn when the middle becomes golden brown. Fry until an even colour is achieved on both sides. Remove the doughnuts from the pan with the slotted spoon and drain on paper towels. Roll the hot doughnuts directly in the black sesame sugar to give a generous coating and repeat with the rest of the dough.

To assemble the doughnuts, mix the tahini and lemon juice into the chilled apricot curd and transfer to the piping/pastry bag fitted with a small plain nozzle/tip. Poke a small hole in the bottom of each doughnut using a skewer or cocktail stick/toothpick and pipe in a generous portion of the curd. Serve the filled doughnuts warm.

KOUIGN-AMANN

Making these fantastic breakfast pastries requires the skill of laminating dough, plus patience and a bit of work. The end results are worth it once you taste the layers of flaky, buttery pastry fresh from the oven. I have made a plain version, but you can choose to serve these with the Matcha Curd (see page 18) or add a filling (see variation, overleaf); for a great surprise centre to this croissant-like delicacy. For best results, make the dough 24 hours in advance to give it plenty of time to rest.

6 g/1 generous teaspoon fresh yeast or 3 g/scant ¾ teaspoon instant dried yeast
1 teaspoon caster/granulated sugar (if using fresh yeast)
130 ml/generous ½ cup warm whole milk
40 g/3 ¼ tablespoons caster/ granulated sugar
250 g/1¾ cups white/strong bread flour, plus extra for dusting
1 teaspoon table salt
1 tablespoon butter, softened
160 g/1½ sticks salted French butter for turns, plus extra for greasing the moulds
200 g/1 cup caster/ granulated sugar mixed with 2 teaspoons table salt for the turns
Demerara/turbinado sugar, for sprinkling (approx. 100 g/½ cup)

stand mixer with a dough hook
12 individual 8-cm/4-inch non-stick tart pans or a 12-hole cupcake pan

MAKES 12 PASTRIES

If using fresh yeast, mix the yeast with the 1 teaspoon of sugar and the warm milk. Leave to dissolve for 15 minutes until frothy. Meanwhile, put the 40 g/3¼ tablespoons sugar, flour and salt in the bowl of a stand mixer fitted with a dough hook. If using instant dried yeast, add this to the bowl now along with the warm milk, or add the frothy fresh yeast mixture and knead for 6 minutes. Add the softened butter and continue to knead for a further 4 minutes. Form the dough into a ball (see **A**, overleaf). Put in a large clean bowl and cover with clingfilm/plastic wrap. Rest in the fridge for 24 hours. The dough will not rise much overnight and this is fine.

The next day, position the salted French butter between two large sheets of non-stick baking parchment. Use a rolling pin to beat the butter into a flat rectangular shape of around 20 × 15 cm/8 × 6 inches. Shape the edges of the rectangle using your hands and try to keep the thickness fairly even. Set aside in the fridge until required.

Bring the salted French butter to room temperature when you are ready to start rolling out the dough. On a very lightly floured surface, roll the chilled pastry into a rectangle of around 30 × 15 cm/12 × 6 inches. Use a pastry brush to dust away any excess flour from the surface of the dough. Put the flattened, room temperature French butter into the centre of the dough rectangle – roughly two-thirds of the dough should be covered by the butter, leaving the edges of the pastry exposed (see **B**, overleaf).

Fold the exposed edges of the dough in on top of the butter then fold the whole rectangle in half. Instead of flour, sprinkle the work surface with the sugar and salt mixture and arrange the pastry on top so that the closed edge is on your right. Roll out the dough again to roughly 1 cm/⅜ inch thick. Fold both edges of the pastry in to meet in the middle, then fold the entire thing in half at the line where the two edges meet as if closing a thick book; this is called a book turn. Wrap the pastry in clingfilm/plastic wrap and chill in the fridge for 20 minutes.

continued overleaf

Roll out the folded dough **(C)** and then repeat the whole process twice more: book fold, use the sugar-salt mixture on the work surface, always start with the closed end to your right and remember to chill for 20 minutes between each fold.

Once the final 20 minutes resting has taken place, grease the tart pans or the cupcake pan with the salted French butter. Roll the dough out for the last time to around 3 mm/⅛ inch thick. Cut into twelve 9 x 9-cm/ 3½ x 3½-inch squares using a sharp knife.

To fold the pastries into the classic kouign-amann shape, tuck in each of the four corners of the square to meet in the middle. (If you are using a filling, add a blob to the middle of each one now.) Put each pastry into a pan or mould **(D)** and sprinkle with a little Demerara/turbinado sugar. Cover loosely with clingfilm/plastic wrap and leave at room temperature to rise for around 2 hours or until doubled in size.

Preheat the oven to 200°C (400°F) Gas 6.

Bake the kouign-amann in the preheated oven for around 15–20 minutes or until the pastry has puffed up and turned golden. Allow to cool slightly, then use a palette knife/metal spatula to remove the pastries from their pans and transfer to a wire rack to cool slightly before serving.

VARIATION

Try adding a delicious filling to these pastries. You could insert a spoonful of matcha custard from the Crunchy Caramelized Custard Buns recipe (see page 46) or a little of the apple compote from the Sparkling Sake Apple Crumble recipe (see page 115) as you leave the dough to rise for the last time.

E

GLAZED BUTTERMILK SCONES WITH KUMQUAT & KINKAN MARMALADE

A quintessential part of British afternoon tea, these scones are extra special. You do need to rest the dough for a while, but they are thoroughly worth the wait. Served with the Kumquat and Kinkan Marmalade (see page 19) or even the Almond Milk and Cherry Blossom Jam (see page 18), they are such a treat for any occasion.

SCONES

250 g/1¾ cups plus
   2 tablespoons plain/
   all-purpose flour, plus
   extra for dusting
15 g/1½ level tablespoons
   baking powder
45 g/3¾ tablespoons caster/
   granulated sugar
50 g/3½ tablespoons butter
90 ml/generous ⅓ cup
   buttermilk
1 egg
30 g/1 oz. sultanas/golden
   raisins (optional)
1 egg yolk, beaten with
   a pinch each of sugar
   and salt, for glazing

TO SERVE

Kumquat and Kinkan
   Marmalade (see page 19)
clotted cream (optional)

*5-cm/2-inch plain round cookie
   cutter*
*baking sheet, lined with
   non-stick baking parchment*

MAKES 8 SCONES

Put the flour, baking powder, sugar and butter in a mixing bowl and rub together using your fingertips. Add the buttermilk and egg, and continue to mix with your hands until combined, being careful not to overwork the dough. The mixture should be slightly sticky but not so much that it sticks to your fingers. Adjust with a little more flour if needed.

If using sultanas/golden raisins, add to the bowl now and knead until just evenly dispersed. Wrap the dough in clingfilm/plastic wrap and rest at room temperature for around 2 hours.

Roll the dough out on a lightly floured work surface to around 3 cm/1¼ inch thick. Stamp out eight rounds with the cookie cutter and re-roll out the scraps to get as many as possible. Turn the dough rounds over so the flat side is facing up. Use a pastry brush to apply the beaten egg yolk glaze and leave uncovered to dry at room temperature for 30 minutes. Repeat the glaze application before leaving again to rest for 1½ hours.

Preheat the oven to 180°C (350°F) Gas 4.

Transfer the scones to the prepared baking sheet and bake in the preheated oven for 8–10 minutes until risen, golden and cooked through. Put on a wire rack to cool. Serve the scones with Kumquat and Kinkan Marmalade and some clotted cream, if you like.

SWEET TARTS

A GOOD TART IS A STAPLE PART OF ANY GREAT PASTRY
CHEF'S REPERTOIRE. IN THIS CHAPTER YOU WILL FIND
TARTS RANGING FROM DELICATE PETITS FOURS, TO
LARGER ONES PERFECT FOR SLICING AND SHARING.
CHOOSE FROM SIMPLE, COMFORTING FILLINGS
LIKE PLUM AND ALMOND WITH SAKE FROSTING
TO CONTEMPORARY PÂTISSERIE FIT FOR SPECIAL
OCCASIONS, SUCH AS THE MISO AND BUTTERSCOTCH.

PLUM & ALMOND TART WITH SAKE FROSTING

A beautiful tart to serve at festive times of the year, and indeed all year round, this dessert has all the makings of a classic Bakewell tart with a few grown up little twists. Japanese plum varieties can actually quite commonly be found in supermarkets throughout the year. I would recommend Methley, Catalina and Elephant Heart, but you can also use more traditional varieties available to you at the time.

TART CASE
½ quantity Sweet Shortcrust Pastry (see page 15)

TART FILLING
1 jar of damson plum jam/jelly, enough to coat the base of the tart
8 large or 12 small plums (see introduction)

FRANGIPANE
250 g/2¼ sticks butter
250 g/1¼ cups caster/granulated sugar
5 eggs
65 g/scant ½ cup plain/all-purpose flour
190 g/scant 2 cups ground almonds
freshly grated zest of 1 orange

SAKE FROSTING
1 teaspoon orange blossom water
300 g/2 cups plus 2 tablespoons fondant icing/confectioners' sugar
30 ml/2 tablespoons sake, plus extra for soaking
pouring cream, to serve (optional)

20-cm/8-inch tart pan
piping/pastry bag with a plain nozzle/tip (optional)

SERVES 8

To make the tart case, prepare the Sweet Shortcrust Pastry following the instructions on page 15. Thinly roll out the flan paste on a lightly floured surface and line the tart pan as neatly as possible.

Trim the edges to fit and then rest the pastry in the fridge for 10–15 minutes. Once chilled, spread a generous layer of damson plum jam/jelly all the way to the edges. Cover with clingfilm/plastic wrap and put in the fridge to chill again while you make the frangipane.

To make the frangipane, cream together the butter and sugar using a hand-held electric whisk until fluffy and well incorporated. Add the eggs one by one and mix until incorporated. Add the flour, ground almonds and orange zest and mix until well combined. Pipe or spoon the frangipane mixture into the chilled tart case on top of the jam/jelly in an even layer, so that the frangipane is level with the top of the pastry. Transfer back to the fridge to rest for a minimum of 30 minutes.

Meanwhile, make the sake frosting. Mix the orange blossom water into the fondant icing/confectioners' sugar, then add the sake, stirring in a little at a time, until you have a thick but spreadable frosting. Cover the bowl of frosting with clingfilm/plastic wrap and set aside until required.

Preheat the oven to 170°C (350°F) Gas 4.

To construct the tart, cut the plums for the filling into quarters and remove the stones/pits and stalks. Remove the tart from the fridge and arrange the plum quarters randomly on top without pressing into the frangipane – you want them to be nestled close together but not on top of each other. Bake the tart in the preheated oven for 40–50 minutes or until the pastry is nicely browned and cooked through. Drizzle over a little sake to taste and allow to soak in as the tart cools in the pan.

Carefully remove the cooled tart from the pan and generously apply the sake frosting to the top using a pastry brush. Allow to set a little before serving slices of the tart cold or warmed through with a little pouring cream on the side, if desired.

MATCHA CRÈME BRÛLÉE TARTS WITH FRESH RASPBERRIES & WHITE CHOCOLATE CREAM

In this dessert the creaminess of the crème brûlée is the perfect match for the earthy matcha, both are beautifully complemented by the fresh raspberries on top. The delicate raspberry tuiles are optional but they make an impressive finishing touch.

TART CASES
½ quantity Sweet Shortcrust
   Pastry (see page 15)
egg yolk for brushing,
   if needed

MATCHA CRÈME BRÛLÉE
1 egg
4 egg yolks
125 g/scant ⅔ cup caster/
   superfine sugar
500 ml/2¼ cups whipping/
   heavy cream
15 g/1¾ level tablespoons
   matcha powder

WHITE CHOCOLATE CREAM
100 ml/½ cup minus
   ½ tablespoon whipping/
   heavy cream
100 g/3½ oz. white
   chocolate, chopped
100 ml/scant ½ cup double/
   heavy cream

RASPBERRY TUILES (OPTIONAL)
100 g/⅓ cup liquid glucose
150 g/1 cup fondant icing/
   confectioners' sugar
20 g/2½ tablespoons
   freeze-dried crispy
   raspberries

TO DECORATE
around 200 g/1 cup
   Demerara/turbinado sugar,
   for glazing
500 g/18 oz. fresh raspberries
icing/confectioners' sugar,
   for dusting

4 individual 8-cm/3-inch tart
   pans
baking beans
sugar thermometer
2 baking sheets, lined with
   non-stick baking parchment,
tuile stencil
small tea strainer
cook's blow torch
piping/pastry bags with small
   plain nozzles/tips

MAKES 4 TARTS

To make the tart cases, prepare the Sweet Shortcrust Pastry following the method on page 15. Thinly roll out the flan paste on a lightly floured surface, then cut into four even squares and line the tart pans. Trim the edges and refrigerate for a minimum of 15 minutes.

Preheat the oven to 200°C (400°F) Gas 6.

Line the cases with baking parchment and fill with baking beans. Blind bake for 12–15 minutes until golden and cooked through. If you spot any hairline cracks then brush the cases with egg yolk and return to the oven for 5 minutes to seal. Remove the parchment and baking beans and leave the tart cases to cool.

To make the matcha crème brûlée, reduce the oven temperature to 150°C (300°F) Gas 2. Whisk together the egg, egg yolks and sugar and set aside. Stir together the whipping/heavy cream and matcha powder in a saucepan and bring just to the boil. Pour the hot cream into the eggs and sugar, whisking constantly until fully combined, thick and creamy. Transfer the mixture to an ovenproof dish and put in a baking pan with high sides. Pour boiling water into the pan to come halfway up the sides and form a bain-marie. Carefully transfer to the preheated oven and bake for 30–40 minutes or until just set with a slight wobble in the centre. Remove the dish from the pan, allow the brûlée to cool and then refrigerate until needed.

To make the white chocolate cream, heat the whipping/heavy cream in a saucepan until just boiling. Remove from the heat, pour over the white chocolate and stir until melted. Let cool a little, then whisk in the double/heavy cream and set aside.

To make the tuiles, put the liquid glucose and fondant icing/confectioners' sugar in a saucepan with the sugar thermometer. Set over medium heat until the temperature reaches 156°C (313°F). Carefully pour the mixture onto one of the prepared baking sheets. Leave to set, then break up and blitz to a fine powder in a blender with the freeze-dried crispy raspberries.

Preheat the oven to 180°C (350°F) Gas 4.

Lay the tuile stencil on the second prepared baking sheet. Use the tea strainer to dust the stencil with an even layer of raspberry–glucose powder. Bake in the preheated oven for 3 minutes or until the sugar has melted. Have a clean rolling pin to hand and remove from the oven. Pick up the paper and carefully lay the hot paper-backed tuiles directly over the rolling pin so that they curve to its shape. Allow to set, then carefully remove the tuiles from the paper. Store in a dry airtight container until needed.

To construct the tarts, remove any skin on the brûlée and whisk until smooth. Generously pipe or spoon the brûlée into each tart case and scrape level. Dust with Demerara/turbinado sugar and heat with the cook's blow torch until golden. Let cool, then arrange the fresh raspberries on top. Pipe the white chocolate cream into the middle and pop a tuile on top, if using. Dust with icing/confectioners' sugar to finish.

VANILLA CUSTARD TART WITH RHUBARB COMPOTE & CRÈME FRAÎCHE

One of the most classic French pâtisserie items, fresh egg custard tarts are also a popular street-food snack in Japan, although their version is closer to the smaller individual Portuguese pastéis de nata. This one is easy to make and a real crowd-pleaser. The sharp rhubarb compote complements the creamy custard perfectly.

TART CASE
½ quantity Sweet Shortcrust Pastry (see page 15)
egg yolk for brushing, if needed

RHUBARB COMPOTE
800 g/28 oz. rhubarb, washed
100 g/½ cup caster/granulated sugar

CUSTARD TART FILLING
500 ml/generous 2 cups whipping/heavy cream
seeds from ½ vanilla pod/bean
75 g/generous ⅓ cup caster/granulated sugar
8 egg yolks
fresh nutmeg, to grate
crème fraîche or sour cream, to serve (optional)

20-cm/8-inch tart pan
baking beans
micro-plane grater (optional)

SERVES 8

To make the tart case, prepare the Sweet Shortcrust Pastry following the instructions on page 15. Thinly roll out the pastry on a lightly floured surface and line the tart pan as neatly as possible. Trim away untidy edges and chill in the fridge for a minimum of 15 minutes.

Preheat the oven to 200°C (400°F) Gas 6.

Line the flan paste with baking parchment and fill with baking beans. Blind bake in the middle of the preheated oven for around 18–20 minutes until golden and cooked through. If you spot any hairline cracks then brush the case with egg yolk and return to the oven for about 5 minutes to seal the cracks. Remove the baking parchment and baking beans and leave the tart case to cool.

To make the rhubarb compote, discard any leaves or roots and cut the rhubarb stalks into 4-cm/1½-inch pieces. Add the rhubarb pieces to a large saucepan with the sugar and 2 tablespoons of water. Give the pan a stir and put over high heat with the lid on. Boil for 4–6 minutes, then drain and transfer the rhubarb to a bowl to cool. Refrigerate until needed.

To make the custard tart filling, put the whipping/heavy cream and vanilla seeds in a saucepan and bring just to the boil. In a separate bowl, whisk together the sugar and egg yolks until pale. Pour the hot cream over the yolk and sugar mixture and whisk until fully combined. Allow the custard to settle then pass through a sieve/strainer to remove any lumps.

Preheat the oven to 150°C (300°F) Gas 2.

If you have a micro-plane grater, then file the rim of the tart shell down to remove the overhang and create a nice clean edge, carefully blowing away any crumbs. Pour the custard into the cooked tart case to fill right to the brim. Grate over the fresh nutmeg and bake in the preheated oven for around 30–40 minutes or until the custard has just set.

Leave to cool completely before using a hot knife to cut the tart into slices and serve with the rhubarb compote and a spoonful of crème fraîche or sour cream on the side, if you like.

BITTER CHOCOLATE, SESAME & CARAMELIZED MISO TART

CHOCOLATE TART CASE
½ quantity Chocolate
Shortcrust Pastry
(see page 15)

MISO CARAMEL
160 ml/scant ¾ cup
whipping/heavy cream
40 g/2 tablespoons liquid
glucose
200 g/1 cup caster/
granulated sugar
3 tablespoons butter
60 g/3 level tablespoons
sweet miso paste

CHOCOLATE TART FILLING
200 ml/generous ¾ cup
whole milk
300 ml/1⅓ cups whipping/
heavy cream
500 g/17½ oz. dark/
bittersweet chocolate,
chopped
3 eggs

SESAME SEED SOIL
100 g/½ cup caster/
granulated sugar
70 g/2½ oz. dark/bittersweet
chocolate, finely chopped
2 level tablespoons white
sesame seeds
2 level tablespoons black
sesame seeds
tempered chocolate shapes,
to decorate (optional)

*20-cm/8-inch tart pan, greased
with oil spray*
baking beans
piping/pastry bag (optional)
sugar thermometer

SERVES 8–10

*Salty miso caramel gives this silky chocolate tart a sophisticated
edge. Serve to guests in small slices as this tart is very rich.*

To make the tart case, prepare the Chocolate Shortcrust Pastry following
the instructions on page 15. Thinly roll out the dough on a lightly floured
surface and line the tart pan as neatly as possible. Trim any untidy edges
and chill the chocolate flan paste in the fridge for a minimum of 15 minutes.

Preheat the oven to 200°C (400°F) Gas 6.

Line the tart case with baking parchment and fill with baking beans.
Blind bake in the preheated oven for around 15–20 minutes or until cooked
through. If you spot any hairline cracks then brush the case with egg yolk
and return to the oven for 5 minutes to seal the cracks. Remove the baking
parchment and baking beans and leave to cool in the pan.

To make the miso caramel, heat the cream in the microwave for around
40 seconds or until just warm and set aside. Add the liquid glucose and the
sugar to a preheated saucepan. Stir constantly over medium heat until you
have a rich, dark caramel. Immediately stir in the butter until melted.
Remove the pan from the heat and gradually pour in the warm whipping/
heavy cream, stirring constantly – do this carefully as the caramel will froth
up. Stir in the sweet miso paste. Allow the caramel to cool a little then pipe
or spoon a layer into the bottom of the baked tart case. Put the tart into
the freezer for around 1 hour or until the caramel has set.

Preheat the oven to 150°C (300°F) Gas 2.

To make the chocolate filling for the tart, put the milk and whipping/
heavy cream in a saucepan and bring just to the boil. Remove from the heat
and pour over the dark/bittersweet chocolate and stir until melted. Whisk
in the eggs and pass the mixture through a fine-mesh sieve/strainer. Pour the
filling into the tart case on top of the caramel and bake in the preheated
oven for 30–40 minutes or until just set in the middle. Leave to cool in
the pan until ready to serve.

To make the sesame seed soil, put the sugar in a saucepan and add
just enough water to make a wet sand consistency. Set over medium heat
with a sugar thermometer inside and heat until the temperature reaches
130°C (266°F). In the meantime, mix the chopped chocolate with the
sesame seeds. Remove the sugar from the heat and stir into the chocolate
and sesame to create a soil-like texture. Tip the soil onto a tray to cool.

To serve, remove the tart from the pan, sprinkle the edges with the
black sesame soil and decorate with tempered chocolate shapes as desired.

YUZU MERINGUE PIES WITH SESAME TUILES

A meringue pie is a true indication of skill for any pastry chef! Zingy,
sharp and fragrant but also indulgent, this recipe is a guaranteed hit.

TART CASES

½ quantity Sweet Shortcrust
    Pastry (see page 15)
egg yolk for brushing, if
    needed

YUZU PIE FILLING

freshly squeezed juice and
    grated zest of ½ lemon
120 ml/½ cup yuzu juice
150 g/¾ cup caster/
    granulated sugar
6 eggs
200 ml/generous ¾ cup
    whipping/heavy cream

YUZU GEL

200 ml/generous ¾ cup
    yuzu juice
1½ tablespoons caster/
    granulated sugar
freshly squeezed juice of
    1 lemon
gellan gum (a quantity that
    is 1% of the weight of your
    mixture – see method)

To make the tart cases, prepare the Sweet Shortcrust Pastry following the instructions on page 15. Roll the pastry out thinly on a lightly floured surface, cut into four even squares and line the tart pans as neatly as possible. Trim away untidy edges and chill in the fridge for a minimum of 15 minutes.

Preheat the oven to 200°C (400°F) Gas 6.

Line the cases with baking parchment and fill with baking beans. Blind bake in the middle of the preheated oven for around 12–15 minutes until golden and cooked through. Remove the parchment and baking beans and leave the tart cases to cool in their pans.

If you have a micro-plane grater, file the rim of the tart case down to remove the overhang and create a nice clean edge, carefully blowing away any crumbs (see **A**, overleaf).

If you spot any hairline cracks then brush the cases with egg yolk and return to the oven for about 5 minutes to seal the cracks (see **B**, overleaf)

Reduce the oven temperature to 130°C (270°F) Gas 1.

To make the yuzu pie filling, whisk all the ingredients together and pass through a fine-mesh sieve/strainer. (Tip: if you want a stronger lemon flavour, do this the day before to allow the zest to infuse fully). Warm the mixture slightly in the microwave for 30 seconds to around 35–40°C (95–104°F) to help the ingredients to combine once in the oven. Pour into the cooked tart cases and bake in the preheated oven for 20–30 minutes or until just set. Remove from the oven and, when cool enough to handle, transfer the tarts to the fridge to cool as quickly as possible to room temperature – this will stop overcooking and therefore cracks appearing.

To make the yuzu gel, combine the yuzu juice, caster/granulated sugar and lemon juice in a small saucepan and heat to boiling point until the sugar has dissolved. Carefully weigh the yuzu syrup mixture in a heatproof bowl and record the result, then put back into the saucepan and reheat until boiling again. Meanwhile, in a separate container weigh out a quantity of gellan gum that is 1% of the weight of the yuzu syrup and mix with the caster/granulated sugar (for example, if the mixture weighs 300 g/10½ oz. you will need 3 g gellan gum). Add the gellan and sugar mixture to the boiling yuzu gel and whisk in. Once completely incorporated, pour into a container and allow to cool and set. Once cool transfer to a blender and blitz until smooth. Set aside ready for constructing the desserts.

continued overleaf

A

B

C

D

MERINGUE
150 g/5¼ oz. egg whites
300 g/1½ cups caster/
  superfine sugar

SESAME & ORANGE TUILES
215 g/1½ cups icing/
  confectioners' sugar
grated zest of 1 orange
65 ml/¼ cup orange juice
65 g/½ cup plain/all-purpose
  flour
65 g/scant ½ cup sesame
  seeds
65 g/½ stick butter, melted
baby basil, to garnish
  (optional)

4 individual 8-cm/3-inch tart
  pans
baking beans
micro-plane grater (optional)
scales that can measure in
  small increments, for the
  gellan gum
stand mixer with whisk
  attachment
sugar thermometer
2 piping/pastry bags with
  a St Honoré nozzle/tip
  and a plain nozzles/tip
baking sheet, lined with
  non-stick baking parchment
cook's blowtorch (optional)

MAKES 4 TARTS

To make the meringue, put the egg whites into the scrupulously clean bowl of the stand mixer fitted with the whisk attachment and put the sugar into a scrupulously clean saucepan. Add just enough water to the sugar to make a wet sand consistency, making sure the sides of the pan are completely clean. Put the saucepan over high heat with a sugar thermometer inside. When the temperature of the sugar reaches 118°C (244°F) begin to whisk the egg whites at a high speed. Take care not to over-whip, they should only be mixed for 3–4 minutes in total. When the sugar reaches hard-boil stage 121°C (250°F) and the egg whites are foamy, reduce the speed on the mixer and gradually pour the hot sugar syrup down the side of the bowl. Be careful not to get any syrup on the whisks or burn yourself. When all the syrup is in, turn the mixer up to full speed and whip the whites to soft peak stage. Lower the speed again and continue mixing until the meringue is cool. Scrape into a piping/pastry bag fitted with the St Honore nozzle/tip and set aside ready for constructing the pies.

To make the sesame and orange tuiles, mix all the ingredients together in a bowl until combined. Cover with clingfilm/plastic wrap and rest in the fridge for 30 minutes.

Preheat the oven to 180°C (350°F) Gas 4.

Using a palette knife/metal spatula, spread the mixture thinly onto the prepared baking sheet and bake for 8–10 minutes or until crisp and golden brown. Set aside to cool ready for serving.

To construct the desserts, pipe the meringue in a wavy line back and forth to cover the entire top of each pie (C), reserving a little to decorate the plates. Heat the meringue gently with the cook's blowtorch to caramelize the top of each (D). Alternatively, you can do this under a hot grill/broiler.

To serve, arrange the pies on your desired serving plates and garnish with piped bulbs of meringue in varying sizes interspersed with piped bulbs of yuzu gel and sprigs of baby basil. Snap the sesame and orange tuiles into rustic shards and arrange them spiking up out of the meringue.

MISO & BUTTERSCOTCH TARTS

These rich and indulgent little treats contain a warming punch of whisky plus a beautiful hit of miso for an umami sweetness. Remember to check the tart cases for hairline cracks, as these will cause filling to seep out. I have made petit four size as they make such great party bites, but you could make bigger ones as desserts too.

TART CASES
½ quantity Sweet Shortcrust
   Pastry (see page 15)
egg yolk for brushing, if
   needed

MISO BUTTERSCOTCH FILLING
100 g/½ cup soft dark brown
   sugar
100 g/1 stick minus
   1 tablespoon butter
1 tablespoon sweet miso
   paste
2 eggs, beaten
100 g/¾ cup currants
50 g/⅓ cup sultanas/golden
   raisins
50 g/⅓ cup raisins
grated zest of 1 lemon
50 g/⅓ cup walnut halves,
   chopped
2 tablespoons Japanese
   whisky (I use the
   Nikka brand)

TO DECORATE
whipped stiff double/heavy
   cream
silver leaf (optional)

*20-hole petit four tart pan
   or 4 individual 8-cm/3-inch
   tart pans*
baking beans
micro-plane grater (optional)

MAKES 20 PETITS FOURS
OR 4 INDIVIDUAL TARTS

To make the tart cases, prepare the Sweet Shortcrust Pastry following the instructions on page 15. Roll the pastry out thinly on a lightly floured surface, cut into 20 even squares and line the petit four tart pans as neatly as possible. Alternatively, cut into 4 squares for individual tart pans. Trim away untidy edges and chill in the fridge for a minimum of 15 minutes.

Preheat the oven to 200°C (400°F) Gas 6.

Line the cases with baking parchment and fill with baking beans. Blind bake in the middle of the preheated oven for around 8 minutes (12–15 for larger individual size) until golden and cooked through. If you spot any hairline cracks then brush the cases with egg yolk and return to the oven for about 5 minutes to seal the cracks. Remove the parchment and baking beans and leave the tart shells to cool.

Reduce the oven temperature to 170°C (350°F) Gas 4.

If you have a micro-plane grater, file the rim of the tart cases down to remove the overhang and create a nice clean edge, carefully blowing away any crumbs.

To make the miso butterscotch filling, put the dark brown soft sugar, butter and sweet miso paste in a saucepan over gentle heat. When melted and combined remove from the heat and let cool to just warm. Whisk in the beaten eggs until fully combined. Add all the dried fruit, lemon zest, chopped walnuts and whisky and stir together. Spoon the mixture into the cooked pastry cases. Bake in the preheated oven for around 10 minutes (or 20 minutes for larger individual size) until the tarts are just set in the middle. Decorate with a small quenelle of whipped stiff double/heavy cream (see page 23) and a little silver leaf for a decadent touch.

LARGE CAKES & GÂTEAUX

THESE SHOWSTOPPING CREATIONS ARE QUITE COMPLEX WITH HIGH FINISHES, HOWEVER THE COMPONENT PARTS CAN OFTEN BE MADE SEPARATELY IN ADVANCE. READ THROUGH EACH RECIPE CAREFULLY BEFORE YOU BEGIN TO GET AN IDEA OF TIMINGS, AS MOST NEED SEVERAL HOURS OR OVERNIGHT TO SET. SEE PAGE 176 FOR INFORMATION ON WHERE TO BUY SPECIALIST MOULDS.

SMOKED CHOCOLATE PAVÉ WITH YUZU GANACHE, MISO & PEANUT BUTTER CRUNCH

This recipe may seem a little daunting but don't be put off. The smoked chocolate element is made simply by infusing cream with a Lapsang Souchong teabag. The yuzu and white chocolate ganache insert will need to be made a day in advance.

YUZU & WHITE CHOCOLATE GANACHE INSERT

250 g/9 oz. yuzu purée

60 g/scant ⅓ cup caster/ granulated sugar

80 g/¼ cup liquid glucose

600 g/21 oz. white chocolate, chopped

2½ large sheets or 5 small domestic leaves of gelatine, soaked in cold water

60 g/½ stick butter, diced

SMOKED CHOCOLATE PAVÉ

1 litre/generous 4 cups whipping/heavy cream, divided in half

2 Lapsang Souchong teabags

500 g/17½ oz. dark/ bittersweet chocolate (63% cocoa)

PEANUT BUTTER CRUNCH

190 g/6¾ oz. milk/semisweet chocolate

50 g/1¾ oz. dark/bittersweet chocolate (63% cocoa)

125 g/4¼ oz. feuilletine flakes (available online) or crushed ice cream waffle cones

75 g/⅓ cup natural peanut butter (I use the Koeze brand)

SWEET MISO DASHI JIRU SAUCE

100 g/6 tablespoons sweet miso paste

2 teaspoons dark soy sauce

Make the yuzu and white chocolate ganache insert a day in advance. Combine the yuzu purée, sugar and liquid glucose in a saucepan over gentle heat until warmed through and the sugar has dissolved. Remove the pan from the heat and add the white chocolate. Stir a little and allow the heat to melt the chocolate gently. Once melted, squeeze the excess water from the soaked gelatine and add to the mixture. Add the diced butter and gently mix everything together. Allow to cool, mixing every few minutes until glossy and smooth. Pour into the 15-cm/6-inch round charlotte ring or silicone insert mould (see **A**, overleaf) and freeze overnight to set.

The next day, make the smoky infusion for the chocolate pavé by putting 500 ml/generous 2 cups of the whipping/heavy cream into a saucepan with the Lapsang Souchong teabags. Set over medium heat and bring just to the boil. Remove from the heat and set aside for 30 minutes to infuse. After 30 minutes, remove the tea bags, squeezing them to release as much of the smoky flavour as possible. Refrigerate the infused cream until needed.

To make the peanut butter crunch, melt both chocolates together in a heatproof bowl set over a saucepan of barely simmering water. Make sure the base of the bowl does not touch the water. Add the feuilletine flakes (or crushed waffle cones) and natural peanut butter and mix with a spatula or wooden spoon until well incorporated.

Spoon the peanut butter crunch mixture onto a sheet of non-stick baking parchment and put another sheet of baking parchment of the same size on top. Use a rolling pin to roll out the mixture gently to about 3 mm/⅛ inch in thick. Transfer the peanut butter crunch (still inside the baking parchment) to the freezer if using immediately or the fridge if making in advance. Note: this will become the base for your dessert so needs to be big enough to fit comfortably underneath the larger silicone mould.

To make the sweet miso dashi jiru sauce, simply mix the miso paste and soy sauce together, then transfer to the piping/pastry bag with the small fine round nozzle/tip and set aside until needed.

To make the mirror glaze, combine the sugar in a saucepan with 3½ tablespoons water and the liquid glucose. Set a sugar thermometer in the pan and take the heat up to 101°C (214°F). Meanwhile, squeeze the water

continued overleaf

A

B

C

D

MIRROR GLAZE

120 g/scant ⅔ cup caster/
  granulated sugar
120 g/generous ⅓ cup liquid
  glucose
4 large sheets or 8 small
  domestic leaves of gelatine,
  soaked in cold water
80 g/⅓ cup condensed milk
120 g/4¼ oz. milk/semisweet
  chocolate
120 g/4¼ oz. dark/
  bittersweet chocolate
  (63% cocoa)

TO DECORATE

tempered chocolate discs
edible gold lustre dust

*15-cm/6-inch round charlotte
  ring or silicone insert mould
20-cm/8-inch round charlotte
  ring or large silicone mould
sugar thermometer
baking sheet, lined with
  non-stick baking parchment
piping/pastry bags with a small
  fine round nozzle/tips and
  a large round nozzle/tip*

SERVES 8

from the soaked gelatine. Remove the pan from the heat once the temperature has been reached and stir in the gelatine. Add the condensed milk and both chocolates. Stir as the chocolate gradually melts and you are left with a shiny glaze. Transfer to a bowl, cover and refrigerate until needed.

To finish the smoked chocolate pavé, bring the infused cream made earlier back to the boil, then pour over the chocolate. Leave for a minute for the heat to melt the chocolate and then stir together. If it looks like it is starting to separate, a little cold cream should help bring it together. Let the mixture cool a little. Meanwhile, semi-whip the remaining 500 ml/generous 2 cups cream to soft peak stage and then fold into the chocolate mixture, being careful not to overwork it. Transfer the finished smoked chocolate pavé to the piping/pastry bag with the large plain nozzle/tip.

To construct the dessert, make sure you have all the components and equipment to hand. Remove the frozen yuzu and white chocolate ganache insert from the freezer. Push it out of the mould, then wrap in clingfilm/plastic wrap and return to the freezer immediately until needed.

Remove the peanut butter crunch from the freezer and remove the top layer of parchment. Put the 20-cm/8-inch charlotte ring or silicone mould on top and use a sharp knife to cut out the base for your dessert. Reserve any crunch shards for decoration, if you like. Transfer the base to the prepared baking sheet and pipe on a generous zig zag of sweet miso dashi jiru sauce, reserving any leftover for garnish. Set aside for a moment.

Pipe a little smoked chocolate pavé into the 20-cm/8-inch charlotte ring or large silicone mould and use a palette knife/metal spatula to smear it into every nook and cranny. Pipe in more pavé to fill about one-third of the way up. Tap the mould on the work surface to remove any air bubbles. Retrieve the ganache insert from the freezer, unwrap and position in the centre of the pavé. Pipe in more pavé around the sides of the insert to fill all the gaps and tap on the work surface again. Add the peanut butter crunch base – with the miso dashi jiru-coated side facing inwards. Scrape the top level and then freeze the whole dessert for at least 3 hours or until set.

Remove the set dessert from the freezer and leave for a moment to come to room temperature. Meanwhile, soften the mirror glaze briefly in the microwave and mix very gently until smooth. It should be at about 30 °C (86°F) to achieve the right consistency. Remove the pavé from the mould (**B**) and put on a wire cooling rack with a tray underneath. Pour the mirror glaze over the pavé from the centre outwards in a circular motion, making sure you cover the whole dessert (**C**). Run a palette knife/metal spatula around the base to smooth over any drips. Transfer to a cake board or serving plate and allow the glaze to set in the fridge before serving.

Decorate using any leftover peanut butter crunch shards or tempered chocolate discs piped with blobs of leftover miso dashi jiru sauce. Spike these into the pavé (**D**) and sprinkle with edible gold lustre dust to finish.

HAZELNUT DACQUOISE WITH SESAME & MISO

This rather elaborate gâteau consists of a traditional nutty meringue-like dacquoise base, adorned with alternate blobs of smooth sesame cremeux (French for 'creamy') and a miso chocolate ganache. The whole thing is layered with two large tempered chocolate discs – you can use the detailed guide to tempering chocolate on page 20 to help you make these. The overall effect is a deliciously rich dessert, with just a hint of saltiness from the miso. The pulled caramelized hazelnuts are an optional decoration, but they lend nicely to the dramatic, contemporary finish.

HAZELNUT DACQUOISE
360 g/12¾ oz. egg whites
120 g/½ cup plus 1½ tablespoons caster/granulated sugar
300 g/3 cups ground almonds
330 g/generous 2⅓ cups icing/confectioners' sugar
60 g/¼ cup hazelnut praline paste
75 g/⅔ cup roasted chopped hazelnuts

SESAME CREMEUX
100 g/3½ oz. egg yolks
50 g/¼ cup caster/granulated sugar
250 ml/1 cup plus 1 tablespoon whole milk
250 ml/1 cup whipping/heavy cream
220 g/7¾ oz. milk/semisweet chocolate, chopped
50 g/¼ cup tahini

MISO CHOCOLATE GANACHE
200 ml/generous ¾ cup whipping/heavy cream
80 g/3½ tablespoons sweet miso paste
200 g/7 oz. dark/bittersweet chocolate (63% cocoa), chopped

continued overleaf

Preheat the oven to 180°C (350°F) Gas 4.

To make the hazelnut dacquoise, use a hand-held electric whisk or stand mixer to beat the egg whites to stiff peaks. Add the sugar gradually, a spoonful at a time, and continue beating until fully incorporated. Carefully fold in the ground almonds, followed by the icing/confectioners' sugar and then the hazelnut praline paste. Finally, gently fold in the roasted chopped hazelnuts. Transfer the mixture to a piping/pastry bag with a large plain nozzle/tip and pipe into the mould or prepared tart pan in an even layer.

Bake in the preheated oven for 15–20 minutes or until a skewer inserted comes out clean. Let the dacquoise cool a little in the pan, then turn out onto a wire rack and set aside. If you have used a silicone mould, it helps to chill the dacquoise in the freezer in order to de-mould.

To make the sesame cremeux, beat together the egg yolks and sugar with a balloon whisk until pale and fluffy and set aside. Combine the milk and whipping/heavy cream in a saucepan and bring just to the boil. Pour the hot cream slowly into the sugar and egg yolks, whisking constantly until fully incorporated. Return the custard to the pan over low–medium heat and cook, stirring occasionally, until thick enough to coat the back of a spoon or until the temperature reaches 82°C (180°F); about 5 minutes.

Meanwhile, melt the chocolate in the microwave or over a bain-marie. Pour the custard into the melted chocolate slowly and mix together using a hand blender until the two are fully combined. Add the tahini and mix with a wooden spoon to incorporate. Transfer the sesame cremeux to a piping/pastry bag with a large plain nozzle/tip and refrigerate until required.

To make the miso chocolate ganache, put the cream in a saucepan and bring just to the boil. Remove from the heat and whisk in the sweet miso paste. Add the chocolate and stir gently with a wooden spoon until melted and fully combined with the cream. Allow to cool, then transfer to a piping/pastry bag with a large plain nozzle/tip, reserving a little for fixing on garnishes later. Note: if the ganache looks like it is going to split, beat briefly with a hand-held electric whisk to bring it together – do bear in mind that it will look more grainy than normal due to the addition of the miso.

A

B

C

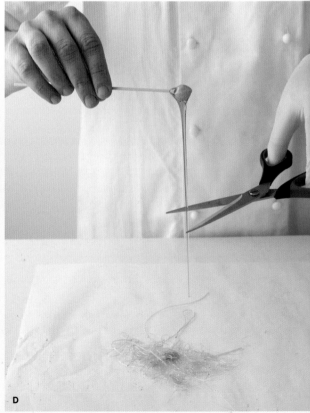

D

CHOCOLATE DISCS
approx. 500 g/18 oz.
tempered dark/
bittersweet chocolate
(see page 20)
plus extra shards of
tempered chocolate
to decorate (optional)

CHANTILLY CREAM
250 ml/1 cup whipping/heavy
cream
250 ml/1cup double/heavy
cream
200 g/scant 1½ cups icing/
confectioners' sugar
seeds from 2 vanilla pods/
beans

PULLED CARAMELIZED
HAZELNUT DECORATION
60 g/3 tablespoons liquid
glucose
200 g/1 cup caster/
granulated sugar
5 whole hazelnuts
(or as many as you like)

*3 piping/pastry bags with large
plain nozzles/tips*
*20-cm/8-inch tart pan, greased
and lined or a silicone mould*
sugar thermometer
hand blender
*Blu-tac and long wooden
skewers, for dipping the
hazelnuts*

SERVES 8

To make the tempered chocolate discs, follow the instructions on page 20 for tempering chocolate, then carefully cut out two 20-cm/8-inch discs.

Make the Chantilly cream just before you plan to construct the dessert: combine all the ingredients in a clean mixing bowl and whisk to stiff peaks.

To construct the dessert, put the dacquoise on a serving plate. Pipe about ten evenly sized bulbs of ganache around the outside edge of the dacquoise, leaving enough space between each for alternating bulbs of sesame cremeux. Fill the gaps with similarly sized bulbs of cremeux so that you have a neat alternating sequence **(A)**. Pipe in a layer of Chantilly cream to fill in the centre and gently put a tempered chocolate disc on top **(B)**. Repeat the piping process on the next layer **(C)** and add the second chocolate disc. Refrigerate the gâteau until ready to garnish and serve.

To make the caramelized hazelnut decoration, put small lumps of Blu-tack on the edge of a work surface spaced well apart (as many as you want to make) and cover the floor with newspaper to protect it. Gently prong each of the hazelnuts onto the sharp end of a skewer and set aside ready for dipping. Have some kitchen scissors to hand.

In a small, very clean saucepan mix the liquid glucose and sugar with 80 ml/⅓ cup water, being careful not to splash up the sides of the pan. Clean the sides of the pan using your finger and some water. Add the sugar thermometer and set over medium heat. Bring the mixture to the boil without stirring. Prepare a separate bowl of cold water that the pan can fit inside. Watching closely, take the temperature up to 155°C (311°F).

When hot enough, very carefully submerge the base of the saucepan in the bowl of cold water for about 20 seconds to halt the cooking process. It is best to have the pan at a slight angle for dipping so remove the pan from the water and put half on top of a folded kitchen cloth.

The ultimate temperature for dipping the hazelnuts is approximately 80°C (176°F). As the caramel cools it will thicken, but you can always return the pan to the heat and warm gently to thin it out again, just don't leave it unattended as it can burn quickly.

When your caramel is at the desired temperature, holding onto one end of a skewer, submerge a hazelnut in the caramel, then remove and carefully push the other end of the skewer into the Blu-tac, allowing the hazelnut to hang over the edge of the work surface and the caramel to slowly drip down. When the drip starts to cool and slows, pull the strand slightly and snip with the scissors to your preferred size **(D)**. Carefully remove the hazelnuts from the skewers before the caramel has set cold; these will keep well for up to 1 day in a dry airtight container. Use small blobs of ganache to fix the caramelized hazelnut decorations to your gâteau in the style of your choosing. You can also add some tempered chocolate shards, if desired.

MATCHA, WHITE CHOCOLATE & CHERRY TRENCH WITH HAZELNUT SPONGE

It is well known that chocolate and cherries are a match made in heaven, throw in matcha to cut through the richness and the flavour combination is elevated to something truly special. The inspiration for this dessert came from a visit I made to Inamura Shozo's cafe in Tokyo, one of the best Japanese pâtisseries. You can make the cherry compote and hazelnut sponge up to a week in advance and freeze them.

HAZELNUT SPONGE
185 g/2 scant cups ground hazelnuts
185 g/generous 1¼ cups icing/confectioners' sugar
5 egg yolks
50 g/generous ⅓ cup plain/all-purpose flour
5 egg whites
25 g/1¾ tablespoons caster/granulated sugar
45 g/3¼ tablespoons butter, melted

MACERATED CHERRY COMPOTE
25 g/1¾ tablespoons caster/granulated sugar
125 g/4½ oz. black cherry purée
125 ml/½ cup kirsch from Morello cherries (below)
3 g gellan gum mixed with with 2½ teaspoons caster/granulated sugar to disperse
250 g/9 oz. macerated Morello cherries in kirsch (I use Griottines), drained

WHITE CHOCOLATE & MATCHA MOUSSE
550 ml/2⅓ cups whole milk
5 tablespoons matcha powder
700 g/24½ oz. white chocolate, chopped

Preheat the oven to 180°C (350°F) Gas 4.

To make the hazelnut sponge, combine the ground hazelnuts, icing/confectioners' sugar and egg yolks in the bowl of a stand mixer with the whisk attachment (or use a hand-held electric whisk) and beat together until well combined. Add the flour and continue whisking until just incorporated.

In a separate bowl, whisk the egg whites to soft peaks, then increase the mixing speed and slowly add the sugar, beating until you have a stiff glossy meringue mixture. Carefully fold this into the hazelnut mixture followed by the melted butter. Spread evenly in a thin layer onto the prepared baking sheet and bake for 10–12 minutes until just cooked and a skewer inserted comes out clean. Turn the baking sheet upside-down onto a wire rack and remove the baking parchment. Leave the sponge to cool.

To make the macerated cherry compote, put the sugar in a small saucepan and mix with a little water to make a wet sand consistency. Set the pan over medium heat and boil without stirring until the temperature reaches 120°C (248°F). When the desired temperature has been reached, remove the pan from the heat and stir in the black cherry purée, followed by the kirsch. Finally add the gellan and sugar mixture and stir to combine.

Bring all the ingredients back to the boil, then mix in the macerated Morello cherries. Pour the cherry compote into the silicone insert mould and freeze for a minimum of 1 hour to set.

To make the white chocolate and matcha mousse, combine the milk with the matcha powder in a small saucepan and bring just to the boil. Pour over the chocolate and leave to stand for 2 minutes before stirring into a smooth ganache. Squeeze out the water from the soaked gelatine leaves and stir into the ganache while still warm. Allow to cool to around 30°C (86°F), then gently fold in the semi-whipped cream. Transfer to the piping/pastry bag and refrigerate until needed.

If you are making the cherry jelly decoration, put the macerated cherry liqueur in a saucepan and bring to the boil. Remove from the heat and stir in the gelatine until dissolved. Set aside ready for decorating the dessert.

continued overleaf

A

B

C

D

6 large sheets or 12 small
  domestic leaves of gelatine,
  soaked in cold water
750 ml/generous 3 cups
  whipping/heavy cream,
  semi-whipped

**CHOCOLATE PISTACHIO
SPRAY (OPTIONAL)**
a store-bought can of green
  velvet aerosol spray (see
  suppliers page 176)
OR if you have a patisserie
  food-grade spray gun:
200 g/7 oz. cocoa butter
300 g/10½ oz. white
  chocolate
green cocoa fat colouring
  (approx. 30 g/1 oz.)

**CHERRY JELLY, TO DECORATE
(OPTIONAL)**
300 ml/generous 1¼ cups
  drained kirsch from
  macerated cherries
  (I use Griottines)
3 large sheets or 6 small
  domestic leaves of gelatine,
  soaked in cold water
macerated Morello cherries
  and tempered chocolate
  shards, to decorate
  (optional)

*baking sheet, lined with
  non-stick baking parchment
scales that measure in small
  increments, for the gellan
  gum
large silicone mould plus
  a small silicone mould
  for the insert (see suppliers
  page 176)
sugar thermometer
piping/pastry bag with a large
  plain nozzle/tip*

SERVES 8

To construct the desserts, make sure you have all the components and
equipment to hand. Remove the frozen cherry compote insert from the
freezer and let it come to room temperature for a moment. Push it out
of the mould, then wrap in clingfilm/plastic wrap and return to the freezer
immediately until needed.

Put your large silicone mould on top of the hazelnut sponge and use
a sharp knife to cut out the base for your dessert. Set aside for a moment.

Use a palette knife/metal spatula to smear the white chocolate and
matcha mousse into every nook and cranny of the mould. Tap the mould
on the work surface to remove any air bubbles. Pipe in more mousse to
fill about half-way up and then tap down on the work surface again.

Retrieve the frozen cherry purée insert from the freezer, unwrap and
position it into the mousse. Pipe in more mousse to fill the gaps around
the edges and then add the hazelnut sponge base. Fill any remaining gaps
with mousse and then scrape level with a palette knife/metal spatula.
Transfer the whole dessert to the freezer for a minimum of 12 hours to set.

Once completely frozen, carefully remove the dessert from the freezer,
let it come to room temperature and then remove from the mould **(A)**.
Wrap in clingfilm/plastic wrap and return to the freezer to firm up for no
more than 30 minutes.

Transfer the dessert to a wire rack set over paper to protect the
work surface and then make the chocolate and pistachio spray, if needed.

To make the chocolate pistachio spray, melt the cocoa butter and white
chocolate together and add enough green colouring to achieve a delicate
light green. Or use store-bought green velvet aerosol spray.

Spray the dessert all over to give an even covering **(B)**.

 If using the cherry jelly to decorate, pour into the recess of the mould
(C) and return to the fridge for 5–10 minutes to set.

Garnish with some leftover macerated morello cherries and some
tempered chocolate triangles, if you wish **(D)**.

LEMON & YUZU VELVET WITH PISTACHIO MACARON

It is really important that you allow yourself enough time to create this beautiful dessert. The yuzu curd insert can be made in advance and will keep well frozen. Make the lemon mousse last when everything else is ready.

YUZU CURD
75 ml/⅓ cup yuzu juice or purée (available online)

2 egg yolks

1 egg

50 g/¼ cup caster/granulated sugar

2 g gellan gum mixed with 2½ teaspoons caster/granulated sugar to disperse

3½ tablespoons butter, diced

a small squeeze of fresh lemon juice, to taste

PISTACHIO MACARON
275 g/1½ cups minus 2 tablespoons caster/superfine sugar

95 g/3¼ oz. egg whites (approximately 3 egg whites)

100 g/1 cup ground almonds

40 g/⅓ cup ground pistachios

137 g/1 cup icing/confectioners' sugar

48 g/1½ oz. egg whites

To make the yuzu curd, put the yuzu juice or purée, egg yolks, whole egg and sugar in a saucepan and whisk together. Set the pan over medium-high heat. As the curd beings to bubble add the gellan and sugar mixture and whisk until boiling and thickened. Transfer the curd to a bowl and stir in the diced butter. Let cool a little, then add a squeeze of lemon juice to taste. Pour the curd into the small silicone mould insert to fill right to the top (reserving the rest for filling the macarons) and transfer to the freezer to set.

To make the pistachio macaron, put the sugar in a saucepan with 100 ml/generous ⅓ cup water and mix until no lumps remain. Set the saucepan over medium-high heat with the sugar thermometer inside. While the syrup is heating, ready the 95 g/3¼ oz. of egg whites in the bowl of a stand mixer with the whisk attachment. When the temperature on the thermometer reaches 110°C (230°F), turn the mixer on and begin beating the egg whites at medium speed. When the temperature reaches 114°C (237°F) and the egg whites have become frothy, slowly and carefully pour the hot syrup down the side of the bowl into the whipping egg whites. Continue to beat on full speed for around 5 minutes until the Italian meringue mixture is cool and looks glossy with soft peaks.

In a clean mixing bowl, combine the ground almonds with the ground pistachios and icing/confectioners' sugar. Add the other 48 g/1½ oz. egg whites and mix with a wooden spoon until incorporated into a stiff paste.

Divide the Italian meringue mixture into two equal portions and set one aside for making the lemon mousse. The other is ready to be added to the macaron paste in three careful stages (if it is over-mixed, it will become too runny and the macarons will not rise). Add one-third of the Italian meringue to the macaron paste and mix in firmly and quickly to ensure there are no lumps. Fold in half of the remaining meringue mixture more gently. Add the rest of the meringue mixture very gently indeed and fold until just incorporated.

Preheat the oven to 140°C (280°F) Gas 1.

Scrape the macaron mixture into a piping/pastry bag with a large plain nozzle/tip. Take the prepared baking sheets and trace the outline of your mould or cake ring on one of the baking parchment sheets. Use some meringue to stick them both onto their baking sheets, pencil-side down for the traced one. Pipe the large macaron in a continuous spiral starting from

continued overleaf

A

B

C

D

LEMON MOUSSE

225 ml/scant 1 cup lemon
 juice
4 large sheets or 8 small
 domestic leaves of gelatine,
 soaked in cold water
half the Italian meringue
 from the macaron (see
 method)
375 ml/ generous 1½ cups
 whipping/heavy cream,
 semi-whipped

TO DECORATE

store-bought yellow velvet
 aerosol spray
 (see suppliers page 176)
OR if you have a pâtisserie
 food-grade spray gun:
300 g/10½ oz. white
 chocolate
200 g/7 oz. cocoa butter
approx. 50 g/1¾ oz. yellow
 cocoa fat colouring
gold leaf (optional)

sugar thermometer
scales that can measure
 in small increments,
 for the gellan gum
large cake ring or round
 silicone mould plus a smaller
 silicone mould for the insert
 (see suppliers page 176)
stand mixer with whisk
 attachment
3 piping/pastry bags with
 2 large plain nozzles/tips
 and a small plain nozzle/tip
2 baking sheets, lined with
 non-stick baking parchment

SERVES 8

the centre and piping outwards until you create a circle just slightly smaller than the template or the cake pan you are using. On the other prepared baking sheet, pipe multiple small macarons; as many as you like. These will be used to decorate the dessert.

Bake both the large and the small macarons in the preheated oven for around 17–19 minutes. The smaller macarons will cook slightly faster than the large one; they are done when they lift easily from the baking parchment, but are still soft in the middle. Remove the baking sheets from the oven and leave the macarons to cool.

To make the lemon mousse, put the lemon juice in heatproof bowl and heat for 20 seconds until warmed through. Squeeze out the excess liquid from the soaked gelatine and stir into the lemon juice. Leave to cool but not set. Once cooled, carefully fold the lemon jelly mixture into the reserved Italian meringue mixture from the macarons. Fold in the semi-whipped whipping/heavy cream and scrape the mousse into a piping/pastry bag with a large plain nozzle/tip, ready for constructing the dessert.

To construct the dessert, make sure you have all the components and equipment to hand. Remove the frozen yuzu curd insert from the freezer and let it come to room temperature. Push it out of the mould, then wrap in clingfilm/plastic wrap and return to the freezer immediately until needed.

Pipe a little lemon mousse into the large cake ring or large silicone mould and use a palette knife/metal spatula to smear into every nook and cranny (**A**). Pipe in more mousse to fill about three-quarters of the way up. Tap the mould on the work surface to remove any air bubbles. Retrieve the yuzu curd insert from the freezer, unwrap and position in the centre of the mousse (**B**). Pipe a little more mousse around the insert to fill any gaps.

Add the large macaron on top to form the base of the dessert (**C**) and again fill any gaps with mousse. Gently tap the mould onto the surface again to get rid of air bubbles and scrape level. Keep any leftover mousse in the fridge to decorate the finished dessert. Transfer the whole dessert to the freezer for 4–5 hours or until the mousse is set.

To decorate, carefully remove the frozen dessert from the mould and put it on a wire cooling rack with paper underneath to protect the work surface. If you have a pâtisserie food-grade spray gun, make the chocolate spray by melting all the ingredients together and transferring to the spray gun. Or use your readymade yellow velvet aerosol spray to spray the dessert in a design of your liking; I have gone for a graduated effect.

Transfer the dessert to a serving plate to let the spray set. Meanwhile, fill the small macaron shells with leftover yuzu curd and sandwich together. Pipe small dots of leftover yuzu curd onto the dessert and use these to fix on some of the small macarons. Finally, add a quenelle of leftover lemon mousse (see page 23) and some gold leaf for a beautiful finish (**D**).

WHITE CHOCOLATE, FRAISE DES BOIS & PISTACHIO DACQUOISE

Fraise des bois translates as 'strawberries from the woods', which refers to wild strawberries, a seasonal summertime treat. I have used a combination of strawberry purée and frozen wild strawberries, which works well. Though quite a complex recipe, the finished item is absolutely stunning and full of summery flavours: a fluffy white chocolate mousse encasing intense strawberry filling and underlaid with a pistachio sponge. You can make the pâte de fruit and wild strawberry compote up to a week in advance and keep them frozen. The mousse and glaze should be made last.

STRAWBERRY PÂTE DE FRUIT

250 g/9 oz. seedless
  strawberry purée
25 ml/1½ tablespoons lemon
  juice
5 g pectin jaune mixed with
  25 g/1¾ tablespoons
  caster/granulated sugar
300 g/1½ cups caster/
  granulated sugar
83 g/¼ cup liquid glucose
¼ teaspoon citric acid

WILD STRAWBERRY COMPOTE

125 g/scant ⅔ cup caster/
  granulated sugar
250 g/9 oz. seedless
  strawberry purée
3 g gellan gum mixed with
  10 g/2½ teaspoons caster/
  granulated sugar to
  disperse
250 g/9 oz. frozen wild
  strawberries
a small squeeze of fresh
  lemon juice, to taste

PISTACHIO DACQUOISE

185 g/scant 2 cups ground
  pistachios
185 g/scant 1⅓ cups icing/
  confectioners' sugar
5 egg yolks
50 g/generous ⅓ cup plain/
  all-purpose flour
5 egg whites

To make the strawberry pâte de fruit, put the strawberry purée and lemon juice in a saucepan with a sugar thermometer over medium-high heat and bring to the boil. Once boiling, turn the heat down, then whisk in the pectin and sugar mixture. Bring back to the boil, then add the sugar and liquid glucose. Whisk everything together to dissolve the sugar, then cook over medium-high heat until the temperature reaches 107°C (225°F). Meanwhile, dissolve the citric acid in a scant teaspoon of water and make sure you have the insert mould to hand. Once the desired temperature has been reached, take the pan off the heat and thoroughly whisk in the dissolved citric acid. Pour the mixture into one of the insert moulds and freeze for a minimum of 24 hours or until required.

To make the wild strawberry compote, put the sugar in a saucepan and mix with enough water to make a wet sand consistency. Add a sugar thermometer to the pan and set over medium-high heat. Boil until the mixture reaches 120°C (248°F). Remove from the heat and add the strawberry purée and the gellan mixed with the sugar. Bring everything back to the boil, then gently mix in the frozen wild strawberries and a small squeeze of lemon juice to taste. Pour the compote into the second insert mould and freeze for a minimum of 24 hours or until required.

Preheat the oven to 180°C (350°F) Gas 4.

To make the pistachio dacquoise, combine the ground pistachios, icing/confectioners' sugar and 5 egg yolks in the bowl of a stand mixer with the whisk attachment (or use a hand-held electric whisk) and beat together. Add the flour and continue whisking until just incorporated.

In a separate bowl, whisk the egg whites to soft peaks using a hand-held electric whisk, then increase the mixing speed and slowly add the sugar, beating until you have a stiff glossy meringue mixture. Carefully fold this into the pistachio mixture followed by the melted butter. Spread evenly in a thin layer onto the prepared baking sheet and bake for 8–10 minutes until just cooked and a skewer inserted comes out clean. Turn the baking sheet upside-down onto a wire cooling rack and remove the baking parchment. Leave the dacquoise to cool and then freeze until needed.

25 g/1¾ tablespoons caster/
granulated sugar
45 g/3¼ tablespoons butter,
melted

WHITE CHOCOLATE MOUSSE
550 ml/2⅓ cups whole milk
seeds from 2 vanilla pod/
beans
700 g/24½ oz. white
chocolate, chopped
6 large sheets or 12 small
domestic leaves of gelatine,
soaked in cold water
750 ml/3 cups whipping/
heavy cream, semi-
whipped

PISTACHIO GLAZE
100 ml/scant ½ cup
whipping/heavy cream
1 generous tablespoon
pistachio paste
(available online)
270 g/9½ oz. white
chocolate, chopped
silver leaf, to decorate

sugar thermometer
large silicone mould plus
2 smaller silicone moulds
for the inserts (see suppliers
page 176)
scales that can measure in
small increments, for the
gellan gum
baking sheet, lined with baking
parchment
piping/pastry bag with a large
plain nozzle/tip

SERVES 8

To make the white chocolate mousse, put the milk in a saucepan with the vanilla seeds and heat until just boiling. Pour over the white chocolate and let the heat from the cream melt the chocolate. Leave to stand for 2 minutes then stir into a smooth ganache. Squeeze out the excess water from the soaked gelatine and stir into the warm ganache. Allow the mixture to cool to around 30°C (86°F), then fold in the semi-whipped cream. Transfer to a piping/pastry bag with a large plain nozzle/tip and set aside in the fridge until needed.

To construct the dessert, make sure you have all the components and equipment to hand. Remove the frozen pâte de fruit and strawberry compote inserts from the freezer and let them come to room temperature. Push both items out of their moulds, then wrap in clingfilm/plastic wrap and return to the freezer immediately until needed.

Put the large silicone mould on top of the pistachio dacquoise and use a sharp knife to cut out a portion the same size, this will form the base of the dessert. Wrap the sponge in clingfilm/plastic wrap and return to the freezer.

Pipe a little white chocolate mousse into the large silicone mould and use a palette knife/metal spatula to smear into every nook and cranny. Pipe in more mousse to fill about half-way up. Tap the mould on the work surface to remove any air bubbles that may spoil the finish of the dessert. Retrieve the inserts from the freezer and unwrap. Insert the frozen strawberry purée insert into the centre of the mousse, followed by the frozen pâte de fruit. Finally add the pistachio dacquoise base. Pipe mousse into all the remaining spaces and then scrape level with a palette knife/metal spatula, making sure the dacquoise is flush with the top of the mould. Transfer the whole dessert to the freezer for at least 12 hours to set.

Make the pistachio glaze on the same day you want to serve your dessert. Combine the whipping/heavy cream and pistachio paste in a saucepan, then stir together and bring to the boil. Remove from the heat and pour over the white chocolate. Stir gently until melted and combined into a smooth glaze. Transfer to a pourable jug/pitcher and leave to cool to room temperature.

Meanwhile, carefully remove the frozen dessert from its mould, wrap in clingfilm/plastic wrap and return to the freezer for 20–30 minutes. Transfer the frozen dessert to a wire rack set over a tray. Pour the glaze gently over the dessert to cover it entirely. Allow the glaze to set (around 2 minutes) and then carefully transfer to a serving dish. Cut into slices to serve and decorate with silver leaf, if desired.

pictured page 92

APRICOT & PISTACHIO ENTREMET

For pastry chefs, the term 'entremet' refers to a dessert consisting of multiple layers in different flavours and textures that complement each other perfectly. I wanted to use a different type of minimal decoration for this (pictured on the previous page) to demonstrate that sometimes the simplest things are the most beautiful; an idea that I feel is synonymous with Japanese culture.

PISTACHIO DACQUOISE
185 g/scant 2 cups ground pistachios
185 g/generous 1¼ cups icing/confectioners' sugar
5 egg yolks
50 g/generous ⅓ cup plain/all-purpose flour
5 egg whites
25 g/1¾ tablespoons caster/granulated sugar
45 g/3¼ tablespoons butter, melted

PISTACHIO CREMEUX
100 g/3½ oz. egg yolks
50 g/¼ cup caster/granulated sugar
250 ml/scant 1½ cups whole milk
250 ml/1 cup whipping/heavy cream
220 g/7¾ oz. milk/semisweet chocolate, chopped
50 g/scant ¼ cup pistachio paste

APRICOT MOUSSE
200 g/1 cup caster/granulated sugar
100 g/3½ oz. egg whites
225 ml/scant 1 cup apricot purée
4 large sheets or 8 small domestic leaves of gelatine, soaked in cold water
375 ml/generous 1½ cups whipping/heavy cream, semi-whipped

Preheat the oven to 180°C (350°F) Gas 4.

To make the pistachio dacquoise, put the ground pistachios, icing/confectioners' sugar and egg yolks in the bowl of a stand mixer with the whisk attachment (or use a mixing bowl and a hand-held electric whisk) and beat together. Add the flour and beat just until fully combined.

In a separate bowl, whisk the egg whites to soft peaks using a hand-held electric whisk, then increase the mixing speed and slowly add the sugar, beating until you have a stiff glossy meringue mixture. Carefully fold this into the pistachio mixture followed by the melted butter. Spread evenly in a thin layer onto the prepared baking sheet and bake in the preheated oven for 8–10 minutes until just cooked and a skewer inserted comes out clean.

Turn the baking sheet upside-down onto a wire cooling rack and remove the baking parchment. Leave to cool.

To make the pistachio cremeux, beat together the egg yolks and sugar with a balloon whisk until pale and fluffy and set aside. Combine the milk and whipping/heavy cream in a saucepan and bring just to the boil. Pour the hot cream slowly into the sugar and egg yolks, whisking constantly until fully incorporated. Return the custard to the pan over low-medium heat and cook, stirring occasionally, until thick enough to coat the back of a spoon or until the temperature reaches 82°C (180°F); about 5 minutes.

Meanwhile, melt the chocolate in the microwave or over a bain-marie. Pour the custard into the melted chocolate slowly and mix together using a hand blender until the two are fully combined. Once combined, mix in the pistachio paste using a wooden spoon. Transfer the cremeux to a piping/pastry bag with a large nozzle/tip and set aside in the fridge until required.

To make the apricot mousse, put the sugar into a saucepan with enough water to make a wet sand consistency. Put the sugar thermometer inside and bring to the boil over medium-high heat. While the syrup is heating, ready the egg whites in the clean bowl of a stand mixer with the whisk attachment. When the temperature of the syrup reaches 118°C (244°F) turn on the mixer and begin beating the egg whites at medium speed.

When the temperature on the thermometer reaches 121°C (250°F) and the egg whites have become frothy, remove the syrup from heat and allow to cool slightly. Slowly and carefully pour the hot syrup down the side

TO DECORATE (OPTIONAL)

a store-bought white velvet
   aerosol spray (see
   suppliers page 176)
OR if you have a pâtisserie
   food-grade spray gun:
200 g/7 oz. cocoa butter
300 g/10½ oz. white
   chocolate
white cocoa fat colouring
   approx. 50 g/1¾ oz.
1 teaspoon each orange and
   green cocoa fat, for flicking
   (optional)

stand mixer with a whisk
   attachment
baking sheet, lined with
   non-stick baking parchment
   or a silicone mat
sugar thermometer
hand blender
piping/pastry bags with large
   plain nozzles/tips
20-cm/8-inch cake pan lined
   with clingfilm/plastic wrap
   or a silicone mould of the
   same size
small food paint brush
   (optional)

SERVES 8

of the bowl into the whipping egg whites. Continue to whisk on full speed until cool and the Italian meringue looks glossy with stiff peaks.

Meanwhile, heat the apricot purée in the microwave for 20–30 seconds until just warm (not hot). Squeeze excess water out of the soaked gelatine and stir into the purée. Leave to cool but not set and then carefully fold the apricot jelly into the Italian meringue. Finally, fold in the semi-whipped cream. Transfer the mousse to a piping/pastry bag with a large plain nozzle/tip ready for building the dessert.

To construct the dessert, cut out a circle of pistachio dacquoise that is the same size as the 20-cm/8-inch cake pan or mould and set aside. Pipe the apricot mousse into the mould or cake pan to fill about three-quarters of the way up, making sure you get the mousse into every nook and cranny. Tap the mould on the work surface to knock out any air bubbles.

Next, pipe in the pistachio cremeux in a layer on top. Add the cut-out circle of pistachio dacquoise sponge and lightly push into the mousse. Pipe the mousse around the outside edge to fill any gaps and then gently tap the mould onto the surface again to get rid of any air bubbles. Transfer the whole dessert to the freezer for a minimum of 4 hours to set.

To decorate, if you have a pâtisserie food-grade spray gun and are making the white spray, melt the cocoa butter, white chocolate and white colouring all separately in either a microwave or over a bain-marie. Mix the white chocolate and the cocoa butter together and add drops of white colouring until you achieve a shade to your liking. Transfer to the chocolate spray gun ready to use; it is very important you do this just before spraying as the chocolate needs to remain warm in order to spray effectively. Alternatively you can use a store-bought white velvet aerosol spray.

Carefully remove the entremet from the cake pan or mould and put on a wire rack. Put some newspaper or cardboard down to protect the work surface and spray all over with the white spray. To create a finish like mine, use a small food paint brush to flick green and red cocoa fat colouring onto the dessert.

pictured page 93

ESPRESSO, FIG & RASPBERRY ENTREMET WITH PINK PEPPERCORNS

This dessert is a real treat for the sophisticated palate, with layer upon layer of flavours to discover. I think that the star of the show is the rich red wine-based compote with pieces of sweet juicy figs and a gentle heat from pink peppercorns and cinnamon. This is enveloped by a silky raspberry mousse and the base is a layer of dark espresso sponge. The whole thing is covered in a sweet fresh raspberry jelly glaze. Feel free to use a round mould for this, if you prefer.

ESPRESSO SPONGE

125 g/4½ oz. egg yolks
112 g/½ cup plus 1 tablespoon caster/granulated sugar
170 g/6 oz. dark/bittersweet chocolate (70% cocoa), chopped
3 tablespoons cold espresso
175 g/6 oz. egg whites

FIG, RASPBERRY & PINK PEPPERCORN COMPOTE

500 ml/2 cups plus 2 tablespoons red wine
360 g/generous 1¾ cups caster/granulated sugar
grated zest of 1 orange
½ cinnamon stick
4 fresh figs, finely diced, plus extra to decorate
500 g/2 cups raspberry purée
225 g/8 oz. fresh raspberries, plus extra to decorate
6 pink peppercorns, chopped
10 large sheets or 20 small domestic leaves of gelatine, soaked in cold water

RASPBERRY MOUSSE

200 g/1 cup caster/granulated sugar
100 g/3½ oz. egg whites
225 ml/scant 1 cup raspberry purée
4 large sheets or 8 small domestic leaves of gelatine, soaked in cold water
375 ml/generous 1½ cups whipping/heavy cream, semi-whipped

baking sheet, lined with non-stick baking parchment
large silicone mould, plus a smaller mould for the insert (see suppliers page 176)
sugar thermometer
stand mixer with a whisk attachment
piping/pastry bag with a large plain nozzle/tip

Preheat the oven to 180°C (350°F) Gas 4.

To make the sponge, use a hand-held electric whisk to beat together the egg yolks and sugar until the whisk leaves a trail; set aside. Melt the chocolate in a heatproof bowl set over a pan of barely simmering water. Do not let the base of the pan touch the water. Fold the melted chocolate into the egg and sugar mixture, followed by the espresso coffee. In a separate bowl whip the egg whites to soft peaks and then carefully fold in. Spread the mixture level on the prepared baking sheet. Bake in the preheated oven for 8–10 minutes or until a skewer inserted comes out clean. Cool in the pan for 5 minutes before turning out onto a wire rack.

To make the compote, combine the wine, sugar, orange zest and cinnamon in a saucepan. Bring to the boil then turn off the heat and let infuse for 20 minutes. Meanwhile, mix the diced figs with the raspberry purée, fresh raspberries and chopped pink peppercorns. Spread into the base of the insert mould. Bring the wine back to the boil, squeeze out the soaked gelatine and stir in until dissolved. Strain the jelly and then pour into the insert mould on top of the fruit to fill. Put the compote into the freezer to set; around 4 hours. Keep the remaining jelly for the glaze.

To make the mousse, put the sugar into a saucepan with enough water to make a wet sand consistency. Add a sugar thermometer and bring to the boil. While the syrup is heating, ready the egg whites in the bowl of a stand mixer with the whisk attachment. When the temperature of the syrup reaches 118°C (244°F) begin beating the egg whites at a medium speed. When the temperature reaches 121°C (250°F) and the egg whites are frothy, remove the syrup from heat and cool slightly. Slowly and carefully pour the syrup down the side of the bowl into the whipping egg whites, being careful not to get any hot syrup onto the whisks. Continue to whisk at full speed until cool and the Italian meringue is glossy and stiff.

Microwave the raspberry purée for around 30 seconds until just warm. Squeeze out the soaked gelatine and stir into the purée. Once this is cool but not set, carefully fold into the Italian meringue followed by the semi-whipped cream. Transfer the mousse to a piping/pastry bag.

To construct the dessert, cut the sponge to the same size as the large silicone mould – this will be the base. Pipe the mousse into the large silicone mould, getting into every corner and filling three-quarters of the way up. Tap the mould on the work surface to remove air bubbles. Remove the compote from the mould and press directly into the mousse, followed by the sponge. Pipe in more mousse to fill all the gaps and scrape level. Tap on the work surface again and freeze the whole dessert for 4 hours until set.

Once set, remove the dessert from the mould and put on a wire rack over a tray. Warm the reserved jelly for the glaze in the microwave to 25°C (77°F). Pour over the dessert and let the excess drip off. Transfer to a plate and refrigerate until set. Decorate with fresh figs and raspberries.

SERVES 8

MATCHA & PISTACHIO OPÉRA

A classic French recipe fused with traditional Japanese ingredients, the sponge for this can be made in advance; the key part is getting the layers just right, but if you manage this, you will achieve a fantastic gâteau opéra. It's quite a lengthy process but you could make the sponge in advance and freeze until needed.

MATCHA SPONGE
185 g/scant 2 cups ground
   almonds
20 g/3½ level tablespoons
   matcha powder
185 g/generous 1¼ cups
   icing/confectioners' sugar
5 egg yolks
40 g/generous ¼ cup plain/
   all-purpose flour
5 egg whites
25 g/1¾ tablespoons caster/
   granulated sugar
45 g/3¼ tablespoons butter,
   melted

PISTACHIO BUTTERCREAM
180 g/1 cup minus 1½
   tablespoons caster/
   granulated sugar
3 egg whites
250 g/2¼ sticks butter, diced
   and at room temperature
50 g/¼ cup pistachio paste

MATCHA GANACHE
150 ml/⅔ cup double/heavy
   cream
1 tablespoon matcha powder
300 g/10½ oz. white
   chocolate, chopped

SOAKING SYRUP
125 g/scant ⅔ cup caster/
   granulated sugar
50 ml/3½ tablespoons
   yuzu juice

continued overleaf

To make the matcha sponge, preheat the oven to 180°C (350°F) Gas 4. Combine the ground almonds, matcha powder, icing/confectioners' sugar and egg yolks in the bowl of a stand mixer with a whisk attachment (or use a mixing bowl and a hand-held electric whisk). Add the flour and beat until incorporated. In a separate bowl whisk the egg whites to soft peaks using a hand-held electric whisk, then increase the mixing speed and slowly add the sugar, whisking until you have a stiff glossy meringue mixture. Carefully fold this into the matcha mixture followed by the melted butter.

Spread the cake batter very evenly onto the two prepared baking pans right to the edges. Bake in the preheated oven for 8–10 minutes until just cooked and a skewer inserted comes out clean. Turn the baking sheets upside-down onto a wire cooling rack and peel off the paper from the bottom of the sponges. Leave to cool on a wire rack until required.

To make the pistachio buttercream, put the sugar in a saucepan with 65 ml/generous ¼ cup water over medium heat with the sugar thermometer inside and bring to the boil. In the meantime, put the egg whites into the bowl of a stand mixer fitted with a whisk attachment. When the temperature of the sugar gets to around 118°C (244°F), turn the mixer on and start to beat the egg whites. When the temperature of the sugar reaches 121°C (250°F) and the egg whites have just reached soft peak stage (take care not to overwhip), reduce the speed of the mixer and very carefully pour the hot sugar syrup down the side of the bowl, being careful not to get any syrup onto the whisks or burn yourself. Increase the speed of the mixer and continue to beat the egg whites for 5 minutes until the mixture has cooled to warm. Gradually add the diced butter and mix until fully incorporated. Lastly, add the pistachio paste and mix in well. Cover the buttercream with clingfilm/plastic wrap and refrigerate until required.

To make the matcha ganache, put the cream in a saucepan with the matcha powder. Stir together and bring just to the boil. Remove from the heat and strain the milk through a fine-mesh sieve/strainer into another bowl containing the chopped white chocolate. Stir gently until the chocolate has melted to form a smooth ganache. Set aside until required.

To make the soaking syrup, put all the ingredients in a saucepan with 75 ml/⅓ cup water and bring just to the boil, stirring to dissolve the sugar. Set aside until required.

PISTACHIO GLAZE

100 ml/scant ½ cup whipping/heavy cream

10 g/½ tablespoon liquid glucose

10 g/generous 1½ tablespoons matcha powder

20 g/generous 1 tablespoon pistachio paste

2 large sheets or 4 small domestic leaves of gelatine, soaked in cold water

270 g/9½ oz. white chocolate, chopped

TO ASSEMBLE

100 g/3½ oz. dark/bittersweet chocolate

stand mixer with a whisk attachment

2 large 24-cm/9½-inch square shallow baking pans, lined with non-stick baking parchment

sugar thermometer

SERVES 12

To construct the dessert, make sure you have all the components to hand. Trim the two sponges into four equal rectangles of around 16 x 12 cm/6 x 5 inches and put one of the rectangles on a large piece of non-stick baking parchment. Melt the dark/bittersweet chocolate either in the microwave or in a heatproof bowl set over a pan of barely simmering water, making sure the base of the bowl does not touch the water. Using a pastry brush, apply the melted chocolate to the first layer of sponge. Allow this to set firm, then turn over; this will form the base of your opéra.

Brush the top of the sponge liberally with the soaking syrup (**A**). Using an angled palette knife, next spread over an even layer of pistachio buttercream (**B**). Put the second piece of sponge on top, brush with more soaking syrup and then use the palette knife to spread over an even layer of matcha ganache (**C**). Put the third piece of sponge on top, brush with syrup and add another layer of buttercream. Add the fourth and final piece of sponge on top and press down lightly with the back of a tray to compress the layers. Brush the top with the remaining melted dark/bittersweet chocolate. Transfer the whole cake to the fridge to set for around 30 minutes; meanwhile make the glaze for the top.

To make the pistachio glaze, combine the cream, liquid glucose, matcha powder and pistachio paste in a saucepan and bring just to the boil. Remove from the heat, squeeze out the excess liquid from the gelatine and stir in. Pour over the white chocolate and stir until melted and combined into a smooth, glossy glaze.

Retrieve the gâteau opéra from the fridge and put on a wire rack over a tray. Pour the warm glaze over the top of the dessert. Smooth over with a palette knife/metal spatula to achieve a nice clean finish and return to the fridge for 20 minutes for the glaze to set.

When ready to serve, trim away the edges of the opera using a serrated knife warmed in a jug/pitcher of hot water (**D**). You can then serve the cake whole or cut into 12 neat slices. Traditionally this cake is decorated with the word 'opéra' piped in chocolate, I have written this in Japanese for an authentic twist and dusted with a little matcha powder to finish. You could also use some silver leaf or delicate chocolate decorations.

DESSERTS

JUST PERFECT FOR DINNER PARTIES, THESE RECIPES
WILL INSPIRE YOU TO GET CREATIVE WITH YOUR
CLASSICS. EVERYONE'S FAVOURITE PUDS ARE HERE:
APPLE CRUMBLE, CHEESECAKE, PANNA COTTA,
PAVLOVA AND CHOCOLATE FONDANT. BUT EACH
WITH AN EXCITING AND DELICIOUS FLAVOUR TWIST.

LAYERED PANNA COTTA WITH SAKE JELLY, FRUIT COMPOTE & CHERRY BLOSSOM

This light, fruity and slightly boozy dessert is the perfect end to any meal.
You will need to make the lychee and raspberry compote the night before serving.

RASPBERRY LYCHEE COMPOTE
200 g/7 oz. fresh lychees
(you can use good-quality
canned, but fresh are best)
4 x 250-g/8-oz. punnets of
fresh raspberries
40 g/generous ¼ cup icing/
confectioners' sugar

PANNA COTTA
425 ml/generous 1¾ cups
whole milk
125 g/4¼ oz. egg yolks
150 g/¾ cup caster/
granulated sugar
3 large sheets or 6 small
domestic leaves of gelatine,
soaked in cold water
250 ml/1 cup crème fraiche
150 ml/⅔ cup whipping/
heavy cream, semi-whipped

SAKE JELLY
100 g/½ cup caster/
granulated sugar
500 ml/2 cups plus
2 tablespoons sake
3 large sheets or 6 small
domestic leaves of gelatine,
soaked in cold water
8 cherry blossoms (optional),
cleaned, soaked in
sweetened water to draw
out the salt and stalks
removed

empty egg box (optional)
8 individual serving glasses
or a large glass dish

MAKES 8 INDIVIDUAL
OR 1 LARGE DESSERT

To make the compote, if using fresh lychees, peel the fruit, cut out the stones/pits and chop into bite-sized pieces. If using canned lychees, cut into quarters and remove the brown tough part, then chop into bite-sized pieces. Mix the lychees with the fresh raspberries and icing/confectioners' sugar in a bowl, then cover with clingfilm/plastic wrap and set aside in the fridge. This will allow the natural colour transformation to take place.

To make the panna cotta, put the milk into a heavy saucepan, set over medium heat and bring to the boil. Meanwhile, in a separate bowl whisk together the egg yolks and sugar. Pour the hot milk slowly into the egg and sugar mixture, whisking well to combine. Return the mixture to the pan over low heat and stir continuously with a wooden spoon until the custard is thick enough to coat the back of the spoon; about 5 minutes. Remove the pan from the heat, then squeeze out the soaked gelatine and stir in until dissolved. Strain the mixture through a fine-mesh sieve/strainer into a bowl. Cover with clingfilm/plastic wrap and refrigerate until cold.

When cold, whisk in the crème fraîche followed by the semi-whipped cream, ensuring no lumps remain. Transfer to a pourable jug/pitcher.

To achieve the slanting design, the panna cotta needs to be set at an angle, so, if using individual glasses, balance the glasses on an upturned empty egg box, making sure they are tilted at the same angle and not going to fall. For a single large panna cotta, put a kitchen cloth into a bigger bowl and use this to support the desired angle of the smaller serving bowl. Pour in the panna cotta to fill roughly two-thirds of the way up the glass and then very carefully transfer the dessert(s) to the fridge for around 4 hours to set.

To make the sake jelly layer, put the sugar in a saucepan with 100 ml/generous ⅓ cup of the sake. Stir over medium heat until the sugar has completely dissolved. Remove from the heat, then squeeze out the soaked gelatine and add to the pan, stirring until dissolved. Stir in the rest of the sake, then transfer to a pourable jug/pitcher and leave to cool but not set.

Meanwhile, if using the cherry blossoms, dip them briefly into the jelly – this will help keep them from floating too much. Position the cherry blossoms around the top of the set panna cotta and carefully pour over the cool sake jelly; if the blossoms still float, gently prod them back down into the jelly. Transfer carefully to the fridge for a further 30 minutes until set.

To assemble the desserts, remove them from the fridge about 15 minutes before you wish to serve. Put spoonfuls of the raspberry and lychee compote on top of the sake jelly along with any juices and serve.

BAKED YOGURT WITH BLOOD ORANGE
& CRUNCHY BROWN RICE

Simple to make, these delicious desserts can be prepared in advance for a visually striking, fresh finish to a dinner party. Alternatively, you could make eight beautiful petit four-sized afternoon tea desserts and serve them in very small dainty glasses.

BLOOD ORANGE COMPOTE
3 large or 4 small blood
   oranges
1 teaspoon cornflour/
   cornstarch
50 g/¼ cup caster/granulated
   sugar

BAKED YOGURT
200 g/scant 1 cup condensed
   milk
200 ml/generous ¾ cup
   whipping/heavy cream
250 g/1¼ cups natural/plain
   yogurt

TOASTED BROWN RICE
50 g/¼ cup uncooked
   brown rice
baby red vein sorrel,
   to decorate (optional)

heatproof serving glasses
piping/pastry bag with a large
   plain nozzle/tip (optional)
large, deep roasting pan
blender (optional)

MAKES 4 INDIVIDUAL
OR 8 PETIT FOUR SIZED
DESSERTS

To make the blood orange compote, peel the oranges and use a sharp knife to cut out the segments, removing any pith. Reserve the segments and squeeze out as much juice as possible from the carcass of the blood oranges into a saucepan.

In a separate small bowl, stir together a tablespoon of the blood orange juice from the saucepan with the cornflour/cornstarch and set aside.

Add the sugar to the saucepan with the full amount of blood orange juice, then set over high heat and bring to the boil. Once the juice is boiling, add the cornflour/cornstarch and whisk constantly until the cornflour/cornstarch has cooked out – give it a taste to make sure that no powder remains. Divide the compote evenly into the bottom of each heatproof serving glass (saving a little for decoration) and let cool. When cool enough, transfer the glasses to the freezer for a minimum of 2–3 hours until frozen, or ideally the night before you want to serve the dessert.

Preheat the oven to 150°C (300°F) Gas 2.

To make the baked yogurt, whisk all the ingredients together and transfer to a piping/pastry bag, if using. Remove the glasses from the freezer and pipe or spoon the yogurt mixture on top of the frozen blood orange compote. Pour a little hot water into the bottom of the large, deep roasting pan and put the glasses into the tray – the water should only come about one-quarter of the way up the side of the glasses. Transfer the bain-marie to the preheated oven and bake for around 10–15 minutes or until set. Remove from the oven and leave the yogurts to cool, then refrigerate until needed.

To make the toasted brown rice, put a small frying pan/skillet over a high heat. Add the brown rice and cook for 3–4 minutes, stirring frequently, until lightly golden all over. Transfer the rice to a heatproof container and, once cooled, crush in a pestle and mortar or whizz briefly in a blender to make a coarse powder. Set aside ready for decorating the desserts.

To construct the desserts, divide the reserved orange segments between each glass on top of the cooled baked yogurt. Drizzle over the reserved blood orange compote and add a little of the toasted brown rice to each. Finish with a little red vein sorrel to dress, if you like, and serve chilled or at room temperature.

VANILLA PANNA COTTA WITH BOOZY CHERRY JELLY & MATCHA MICRO SPONGE

PANNA COTTA
600 ml/2⅔ cups whipping/
  heavy cream
180 ml/¾ cup whole milk
seeds from 3 vanilla pods/
  beans
90 g/scant ½ cup caster/
  granulated sugar
2 large sheets or 4 small
  domestic leaves of gelatine,
  soaked in cold water
silver leaf, to decorate
  (optional)

CHERRY GEL & COMPOTE
200 ml/generous ¾ cup
  drained macerated
  Morello cherry liqueur
  (I use Griottines)
2 g gellan gum mixed with
  1½ tablespoons caster/
  granulated sugar to
  disperse
20–30 macerated Morello
  cherries (taken from jar
  above)

MATCHA MICRO SPONGE
80 g/generous ⅓ cup caster/
  granulated sugar
210 g/1½ cups cake flour
  (or use plain/all-purpose
  flour if not available)
240 g/8½ oz. egg whites
20 g/3½ level tablespoons
  matcha powder
50 g/generous ⅓ cup icing/
  confectioners' sugar

4 dariole moulds
scales that can measure in
  small increments, for the
  gellan gum
espuma gun and polystyrene
  cup, for the micro sponge

MAKES 4 DESSERTS

This recipe for panna cotta is very versatile and you can swap the fruit accompaniment seasonally, a strawberry compote in summer would work beautifully. I find that jarred Griottine cherries give the best flavour because they are aged, but you could also use fresh cherries soaked in kirsch liqueur.

To make the panna cotta, put the whipping/heavy cream, milk, vanilla seeds and sugar in a saucepan and bring to the boil over medium heat. Remove from the heat, squeeze the water from the soaked gelatine and stir into the cream until dissolved. Pour the panna cotta mixture into a bowl and put inside a larger bowl filled with ice to cool. When the mixture is cool and just beginning to set, give it a whisk then divide between the dariole moulds. Transfer to the fridge for a minimum of 2–3 hours or until completely set.

To make the cherry gel and compote, put the macerated Morello cherry liqueur into a saucepan and bring to the boil. Add the gellan and sugar mixture to the boiling liqueur and whisk until dissolved. Pour into a container to cool and refrigerate for 15 minutes or until set. Once completely set, blitz to a very fine gel in a food processor. If the gel seems overly thick, add some more cherry liqueur to loosen. Set aside in the fridge until ready to serve.

To make the matcha micro sponge, mix all the ingredients together and fill into a syphon or espuma gun and gas twice. Once the gas has been added, squeeze into a polystyrene cup and microwave for 40 seconds. Remove from the microwave and cut into large pieces. Set aside for plating.

To construct the desserts, put a tablespoon of cherry gel on each serving plate and quickly smear across using a palette knife/metal spatula or butter knife, set aside for a moment. Add the leftover gel to the macerated Morello cherries and mix together to create the cherry compote.

Quickly submerge the panna cotta moulds in warm water to help loosen and gently turn them out onto the centre of each serving plate, about half-way across the smear of cherry gel. Add the micro sponge to the plates and dress with a little cherry compote. Finish with silver leaf for a decadent touch, if you like.

WHITE SESAME & ADZUKI BEAN CHEESECAKE WITH TAHINI & CHOCOLATE SESAME SOIL

Cheesecake is always a crowd-pleaser, this one consists of a traditional biscuit base topped with a rich, nutty cream and finished with a dark/bittersweet chocolate 'soil'. You can make the koshian (adzuki bean paste) from scratch following my recipe, or buy it online or from a specialist Japanese store if pressed for time.

CHEESECAKE BASE
200 g/7 oz. digestive biscuits/
  graham crackers
100 g/1 stick minus
  1 tablespoon butter,
  melted and cooled

CHEESECAKE MIXTURE
350 g/generous 1½ cups
  cream cheese
150 ml/⅔ cup crème fraîche
seeds from 2 vanilla pods/
  beans
100 g/½ cup tahini, plus extra
  to decorate
100 g/½ cup koshian paste
  (store-bought or see
  recipe page 19)
2 large sheets or 4 small
  domestic leaves of gelatine,
  soaked in cold water
4 egg whites
a pinch of salt
100 g/½ cup caster/
  granulated sugar

CHOCOLATE & SESAME SOIL
100 g/½ cup caster/
  granulated sugar
70 g/2½ oz. dark/bittersweet
  chocolate, finely chopped
1½ tablespoons each white
  and black sesame seeds

*20-cm/8-inch round springform
  cake pan, lined with
  clingfilm/plastic wrap
  or a silicone mould
sugar thermometer
piping/pastry bag with a small
  nozzle/tip (optional)*

SERVES 8

To make the cheesecake base, roughly crumble the digestive biscuits/graham crackers with your fingers so they are broken into a rubble. Stir in the melted and slightly cooled butter until well combined. Press evenly into the base of the pan or mould and then refrigerate until required.

To make the cheesecake mixture, put the cream cheese, crème fraîche, vanilla seeds, tahini and koshian paste in a large mixing bowl and cream together using a hand-held electric whisk.

Warm a couple of tablespoons of the cheesecake mixture in the microwave for 20 seconds, then squeeze out the excess water from the soaked gelatine and stir into the small amount of warm cheesecake mixture until dissolved. Set aside.

In a separate bowl, use a hand-held electric whisk to beat the egg whites to soft peaks. Slowly add the salt and sugar, whisking at high speed, until fully combined and you have a stiff, glossy meringue mixture.

Stir the dissolved gelatine into the large bowl of cheesecake mixture and then fold in the meringue until fully incorporated. Pour into the pan or silicone mould on top of the chilled base and refrigerate for around 3 hours or overnight until the cheesecake has set.

To make the chocolate and sesame soil, put the sugar in a saucepan and add enough water to make a wet sand consistency. Put the sugar thermometer in the pan and set over medium heat for a few minutes until the temperature reaches 130°C (266°F).

Meanwhile, in a separate bowl, mix the chopped chocolate with the sesame seeds. When the sugar is at the desired temperature, remove from the heat and whisk in the chocolate and sesame seeds; this will create the 'soil' texture. Tip out onto a tray to cool.

To construct the dessert, remove the set cheesecake from the pan or mould and put onto a serving plate. Add chocolate soil to the top in the centre and finish by piping over some dots of tahini.

KINKAN MARMALADE CREAM WITH YOGURT TUILES, PEANUT & SESAME NOUGATINE

YOGURT TUILES

75 g/generous ½ cup fondant
   icing/confectioners' sugar
2½ tablespoons liquid
   glucose
40 g/3¼ tablespoons acidic
   yogurt powder

MARMALADE CREAM

350 g/1½ cups cream cheese
190 ml/¾ cup double/heavy
   cream
60 g/scant ⅓ cup caster/
   granulated sugar
seeds from 1 vanilla pod/bean
50 g/3 tablespoons Kumquat
   and Kinkan Marmalade
   (see recipe page 19 or use
   store-bought)

PEANUT NOUGATINE

100 g/½ cup caster/
   granulated sugar
50 g/⅓ cup salted peanuts
30 g/¼ cup mixed black and
   white sesame seeds
4 digestive biscuits/graham
   crackers

KUMQUAT & YUZU CURD

1 egg, plus 2 yolks
50 g/¼ cup caster/
   granulated sugar
squeeze of fresh lemon juice
60 ml/¼ cup yuzu juice or
   purée (available online)
2 tablespoons juice from
   Kumquat and Kinkan
   Marmalade (see above)
3½ tablespoons butter, diced
pieces of kumquat from the
   marmalade, decorate

sugar thermometer
3 baking sheets, lined with
   non-stick baking parchment
piping/pastry bags

SERVES 4

A deconstructed cheesecake of sorts, practise your plating skills and guests will not fail to be impressed with this grown-up dessert. You can make the yogurt tuiles a few days in advance and they will keep well stored in a dry airtight container.

To make the yogurt tuiles, combine the fondant icing/confectioners' sugar and liquid glucose in a saucepan and add the sugar thermometer. Heat until the temperature reaches 156°C (313°F). Pour the hot syrup carefully onto the first prepared baking sheet. Allow the mixture to cool completely until set, then break up and blitz to a fine powder in a food processor. Add the acidic yogurt powder and blend again.

Preheat the oven to 180°C (350°F) Gas 4.

Evenly dust the powder over the second prepared baking sheet. Bake in the preheated oven for 3–4 minutes or until the sugar has melted. Remove from the oven and allow to cool. Break into rustic shards. Store the tuiles in a dry airtight container, ready for decorating the desserts.

To make the marmalade cream, beat together all the ingredients using a balloon whisk until you have a thick mixture. Transfer to a container and refrigerate until needed.

To make the nougatine, preheat a large, dry frying pan/skillet. Add the sugar and stir with a wooden spoon until it turns into a nice dark caramel. Add the salted peanuts and sesame seeds and mix to coat in the caramel. Pour onto the third lined baking sheet and allow to cool and set. Break the nougatine into shards and put in a food processor with the digestive biscuits/graham crackers. Pulse briefly (but don't overblend) to form a rough crumbly mixture. Store in a dry container until needed.

To make the kumquat and yuzu curd, put the whole egg, egg yolks, sugar, lemon juice, yuzu juice or purée and marmalade juice in a large saucepan and stir together. Bring to the boil, whisk constantly, and let boil for around 2–3 minutes, whisking, until the consistency has thickened.

Remove from the heat and transfer the curd to a bowl. Stir in the diced butter and mix every few minutes until melted and completely incorporated. Let cool, then transfer to a piping/pastry bag with a small nozzle/tip.

To construct the desserts, spread a tablespoon of nougatine crumbs across each serving plate in a slightly curved shape. Follow the instructions for quenelling on page 23 and make three neat quenelles of marmalade cream to put down the centre of each. Add some of the kumquat pieces from the marmalade and pipe small dots of kumquat and yuzu curd around the plates. Finish by placing a shard of yogurt tuile into each of the three quenelles of marmalade cream.

SPARKLING SAKE APPLE CRUMBLE

This twist on the classic dessert is a little tweak on the very successful apple dish that we made for The Great British Bake off: Crème de la Crème.

SAKE PARFAIT & SAUCE
240 g/8¼ oz. egg yolks
   (about 12 yolks)
225 g/1 cup plus
   2 tablespoons caster/
   superfine sugar
100 ml/⅓ cup liquid glucose
100 ml/⅓ cup sparkling sake,
   plus extra to taste
190 g/¾ cup crème fraîche
120 g/½ cup whipping/heavy
   cream, whipped
icing/confectioners' sugar,
   to dust

SPECULOOS CRUMBLE
400 g/3 cups plain/
   all-purpose flour
3 tablespoons ground
   cinnamon
2 tablespoons each ground
   ginger and nutmeg
1 tablespoon baking powder
200 g/1 cup light brown
   muscovado sugar
60 ml/¼ cup whole milk
300 g/2¾ sticks butter

APPLE COMPOTE
2 cooking apples (such as
   Bramleys) and 2 Asian
   nashi pears, peeled,
   cored and diced
100 g/½ cup caster/
   granulated sugar
freshly squeezed juice
   of 1 lemon
½ teaspoon toasted,
   crushed fennel seeds

stand mixer with a whisk
   attachment
sugar thermometer
8 silicone insert moulds
serving glasses

MAKES 8 DESSERTS

To make the sake parfait and sauce, first make a sabayon. Begin to whisk the egg yolks in the bowl of a stand mixer on medium speed. Meanwhile, put the sugar and liquid glucose in a saucepan and stir in enough water to make a wet sand consistency. Add the sugar thermometer and make sure the edge of the saucepan is completely clean. Set over high heat and take the temperature up to 118°C (244°F). When the temperature has been reached and the egg yolks are frothy, slowly pour the hot syrup into the egg yolks, whisking at low speed and being careful not to get any syrup onto the whisks. Increase the speed and whisk for 10–15 minutes until the mixture has doubled in volume. Reduce the speed again and whisk until cool.

Split the sabayon into two equal portions and set one portion aside in a covered bowl in the fridge. To the other, add the sparkling sake, crème fraîche and whipped cream to make the parfait. Stir together and pour into the eight silicone insert moulds. Freeze for a minimum of 6 hours or overnight until frozen solid.

Preheat the oven to 180°C (350°F) Gas 4.

To make the speculoos crumble, mix all the ingredients together in a bowl and bring together to form a dough. Refrigerate for 10 minutes until chilled and firm. When ready, roll out the dough to an even thickness between two sheets of non-stick baking parchment. Remove the top layer of parchment, put on a baking sheet and bake in the preheated oven for 15 minutes or until golden brown. Remove from the oven and leave to cool.

To make the apple compote, put the diced apples and pears into a saucepan. Add the sugar, lemon and toasted, crushed fennel seeds. Cook over low heat until the fruit starts to break down but still has a little bite.

To construct the desserts, remove the parfaits from the moulds and return to the freezer wrapped in clingfilm/plastic wrap. Break the speculoos into smallish pieces. Warm the reserved sabayon and add sparkling sake to taste (along with a little cream if you like it richer). Transfer to a serving bowl or jug/pitcher. Have serving glasses at the ready. Warm the apple compote through, if needed, and spoon half into the bottom of the glasses. Retrieve the frozen parfaits, unwrap and position in the centre of each glass, adding the rest of the apple compote on top. Finally, add the speculoos crumble and dust with icing/confectioners' sugar. Serve immediately with the warm sake sauce on the side.

Note This dessert can be served warm or cold: if serving warm, ensure the parfaits are frozen as hard as possible first, then quickly build and serve the dessert immediately – your guests will love the contrast in temperature.

EARL GREY, LEMON, SULTANA & CARAMELIZED BRIOCHE DESSERTS WITH IRISH CREAM LIQUEUR

This is a recipe that is very dear to me and has featured on many of my dessert menus throughout the years in various incarnations. I suggest you buy some good-quality brioche to form the casing to save time. However, if you want to make it yourself, you can always contact me on Twitter @dessertdoctor where I will be happy to provide you with a recipe. If needed, the brûlée and compote can be made a day in advance.

NOUGATINE DECORATION
100 g/½ cup caster/
  granulated sugar
50 g/⅔ cup flaked/slivered
  almonds

**IRISH CREAM LIQUEUR
BRÛLÉE**
70 ml/scant ⅓ cup Irish
  cream liqueur
  (such as Baileys)
190 ml/generous ¾ cup
  whipping/heavy cream
190 ml/generous ¾ cup
  double/heavy cream
5 egg yolks
60 g/scant ⅓ cup caster/
  granulated sugar

LEMON & SULTANA COMPOTE
100 g/¾ cup golden sultanas
1 Earl Grey teabag
150 g/generous 1 cup
  sultanas
60 g/scant ⅓ cup caster/
  granulated sugar
freshly squeezed juice
  of 1 lemon

First make the nougatine decoration. Preheat a dry saucepan. Add the sugar gradually, a spoonful at a time, and stir with a wooden spoon until melted into a dark caramel. Add the flaked/slivered almonds and stir to coat in the caramel. Pour the mixture onto the prepared baking sheet and allow to cool until set.

Preheat the oven to 180°C (350°F) Gas 4.

Blitz the cooled and set nougatine in a food processor to a fine powder and then use a fine-mesh sieve/strainer to dust a delicate layer over a silicone mat. Use the 5-cm/2-inch cutter to press down to make four square shapes, shuffling the cutter to make a sizeable gap (see **A**, overleaf). Bake in the preheated oven for about 3–4 minutes until melted; don't discard the outside edges as these will be used as decorations too. Store the nougatine decorations in a dry airtight container until needed.

To make the Irish cream liqueur brûlée combine the Irish cream liqueur, whipping/heavy cream and double/heavy cream in a saucepan and bring to the boil over medium heat. Meanwhile, whisk the egg yolks and sugar together in a separate bowl using a hand-held electric whisk. Pour the hot cream mixture slowly into the yolks and sugar, whisk constantly until fully incorporated. Strain the mixture through a fine-mesh sieve/strainer and allow to settle for around 10 minutes.

Preheat the oven to 150°C (300°F) Gas 2.

Skim off any foam that has settled on top of the brûlée and transfer the mixture to a baking dish. Place the dish inside a baking tray and fill half-way up the sides of the dish with boiling water to create a bain-marie. Bake in the preheated oven for around 35–50 minutes or until set. (Keep checking as the cooking time depends a lot on your oven.) Allow to cool, then refrigerate the brûlée until required.

To make the lemon and sultana compote, put the golden sultanas in a large saucepan, cover with water and boil for 20 minutes to plump the fruit. Remove the pan from the heat and add the Earl Grey teabag. Leave to infuse for a maximum of 20 minutes, then remove the teabag and set the pan aside.

continued overleaf

BRIOCHE CUBES
a whole loaf of good-quality
    unsliced brioche
olive oil, for brushing
icing/confectioners' sugar,
    for dusting

EARL GREY GANACHE
100 ml/scant ½ cup
    whipping/heavy cream
2 Earl Grey teabags
100 g/3½ oz. milk/semisweet
    chocolate, chopped

*baking sheet, lined with
    non-stick baking parchment*
silicone mat
*5-cm/2-inch square metal
    cutter*
*2 piping/pastry bags with a
    star-shaped size 2 nozzle/tip
    and a plain nozzle/tip*

MAKES 4 DESSERTS

In a clean saucepan, stir together the sultanas with the sugar, lemon juice and 180 ml/¾ cup water and bring to the boil. Turn down the heat and gently simmer everything for 20 minutes. Remove the pan from the heat, let the mixture cool slightly and then blend in a food processor to a smooth purée. Drain the soaked tea-infused sultanas and mix into the purée to give a nice compote consistency. Set aside.

Preheat the oven to 220°C (425°F) Gas 7.

To make the brioche cubes, cut the brioche loaf into 5 cm/2 inch wide pieces and trim the edges to make four 5 cm/2 inch square cubes. Brush all sides of the cubes with olive oil and dust all the edges with icing/confectioners' sugar. Put the cubes on a baking sheet and bake in the preheated oven for 10 minutes, turning once half-way through, if needed, until perfectly browned all round. Remove from the oven and leave to cool completely on a wire rack.

Once cool, use a small sharp knife to cut a 3-cm/1-inch square in one side of each brioche **(B)**, reaching about three-quarters of the way inside each cube. Carefully remove the middle of each square and discard, leaving a neat hollow pocket with a sturdy base. Set aside.

To make the Earl Grey ganache, put the whipping/heavy cream in a saucepan and set over medium heat until warmed through. Put the Earl Grey teabags in the cream and allow to infuse for 20 minutes. Squeeze the teabags out thoroughly and discard. Put the cream in a saucepan and bring just to the boil. Pour over the milk/semisweet chocolate and stir gently to form a smooth ganache. Transfer to the fridge to firm up until the ganache is a pipeable consistency. Scrape into the piping/pastry bag with the star-shaped size 2 nozzle/tip and set aside for finishing the dessert.

To construct the desserts, whisk the brûlée and transfer to the piping/pastry bag with the plain nozzle/tip. Put a heaped teaspoon of lemon and Earl Grey compote in the bottom of each and then pipe in Irish cream liqueur brûlée to fill just to the top. Pipe dots of Earl Grey ganache around the top edge of the brioche **(C)** and then gently position a square of nougatine on top **(D)**. Pipe a larger bulb of ganache in the centre of the nougatine square and add a shard of leftover nougatine to the top. Serve with any leftover compote.

PASSION FRUIT PAVLOVA, WITH MOMO FRUIT & PINK PEPPERCORN SUGAR

PAVLOVA
4 egg whites
140 g/¾ cup minus
    2 teaspoons caster/
    granulated sugar
140 g/1 cup icing/
    confectioners' sugar, sifted
1 teaspoon cornflour/
    cornstarch

PASSION FRUIT CURD
50 g/1¾ oz. passion fruit pulp
1 whole egg, plus 2 egg yolks
50 g/¼ cup caster/granulated
    sugar
3½ tablespoons butter, diced

MACERATED MOMO FRUIT
2 large or 3 small momo
    peaches
100 g/½ cup caster/
    granulated sugar
5 pink peppercorns
1 cinnamon stick
1 whole passion fruit
1 bay leaf
80 ml/⅓ cup orange liqueur
    (such as Grand Marnier)

CHANTILLY CREAM
100 ml/scant ½ cup each
    whipping/heavy cream
    and double/heavy cream
seeds from 1 vanilla pod/bean
1 tablespoon icing/
    confectioners' sugar

PINK PEPPERCORN SUGAR
¾ tablespoon pink
    peppercorns, ground with
    50 g/¼ cup white sugar

stand mixer with a whisk
    attachment
piping/pastry bags with a large
    and a small plain nozzle/tip
baking sheet, lined with
    non-stick baking parchment

MAKES 4 DESSERTS

Momo fruit is a type of Japanese peach, usually larger and softer than Western varieties. This, along with a zingy passion fruit curd, provides a delicate contemporary twist on a much-loved classic.

Preheat the oven to 100°C (215°F) Gas ¼.

To make the pavlovas, beat the egg whites in the scrupulously clean bowl of a stand mixer at medium speed until doubled in volume. Add the sugar, a spoonful at a time, and whisk at high speed for 10 minutes. The mixture may seem over-whipped but that is perfect for this recipe.

Combine the icing/confectioners' sugar with the cornflour/cornstarch in a separate bowl and fold gently into the meringue mixture in three stages.

Transfer the mixture to a piping/pastry bag with the large nozzle/tip and pipe four equally sized individual meringues (about 10 cm/4 inches in diameter) on the prepared baking sheet. Drag a small palette knife/metal spatula up the sides of each meringue from the bottom to the top a few times to form a peak. Bake in the preheated oven for around 1 hour or until the pavlovas lift easily from the baking sheet. Set aside to cool.

To make the curd, combine all the ingredients (apart from the butter) in a saucepan and whisk together over medium heat. Whisk the boiling mixture constantly until thickened. Transfer to a bowl and add the butter. Whisk occasionally as the mixture cools, then refrigerate until needed.

To make the macerated momo fruit, cut the peaches into wedges and remove the stones/pits. Put the fruit in a large heatproof bowl. Stir together all the other ingredients with 100 ml/⅓ cup water in a saucepan and bring to the boil. If the peach flesh is ripe you can simply pour the boiling liquid over, cover with clingfilm/plastic wrap and leave to cool. If the peaches are hard, add them to the poaching liqueur and simmer until softened but not broken down, discarding any skin that falls off. Allow the mixture to cool.

To make the Chantilly cream, whisk all the ingredients together with a hand-held electric mixer until soft peaks form; refrigerate until required.

To construct the desserts, remove the peaches from the poaching liqueur and drain on paper towels. At this point you can strain and then heat the remaining poaching liqueur in a saucepan over high heat for 5 minutes until reduced, to serve as a sauce with the pavlovas, if you wish.

Put the pavlovas on suitable serving plates and whip the Chantilly cream to firm peaks. Spoon or pipe some Chantilly cream onto each meringue, and then pipe or spoon over the passion fruit curd. Pile some macerated momo fruit on top of each and drizzle with the reduced sauce, if using. Finally lightly dust the pavlovas with the pink peppercorn sugar, to serve.

SANSHO PEPPERCORN & STRAWBERRY ETON MESS WITH MATCHA MERINGUES & YUZU

Here is a simple but inventive twist on a classic much-loved dessert, perfect for impressing friends at a dinner party. I feel this is a good amount of pepper to create a gentle heat, but you can add more if you want a punchier kick.

SANSHO STRAWBERRIES

500 g/18 oz. fresh
   strawberries, hulled
   and quartered
2 tablespoons icing/
   confectioners' sugar
sansho peppercorns
   in a grinder

MERINGUES

4 egg whites
140 g/scant ¾ cup caster/
   superfine sugar
140 g/1 cup icing/
   confectioners' sugar, sifted
2 tablespoons matcha
   powder, to dust

YUZU CURD

75 ml/⅓ cup yuzu juice
   or purée
2 egg yolks
1 egg
50 g/¼ cup caster/
   granulated sugar
3½ tablespoons butter, diced
a small squeeze of fresh
   lemon juice, to taste

WHITE CHOCOLATE CREAM

100 ml/scant ½ cup
   whipping/heavy cream
100 g/3½ oz. white
   chocolate, chopped
100 ml/scant ½ cup double/
   heavy cream
shisho cress, to decorate

*stand mixer with a whisk
   attachment*
*2 piping/pastry bags with a size
   8 and a size 4 nozzle/tip*
*baking sheet, lined with
   non-stick baking parchment*

To make the sansho strawberries, mix together the strawberries, icing/confectioners' sugar and four grinds of the sansho peppercorns. Taste to check you are happy with the amount of pepper and set aside in the fridge until needed.

Preheat the oven to 110°C (225°F) Gas ¼.

To make the meringues, put the egg whites in the bowl of a stand mixer with the whisk attachment and beat at a high speed until doubled in size. Gradually add the caster/superfine sugar and continue to beat the egg whites at high speed for around 10 minutes. Don't worry if you think the mixture looks over-whipped, that is perfect for this recipe.

Fold the icing/confectioners' sugar into the egg whites in three parts until fully incorporated. Scrape the mixture into the piping/pastry bag with the size 8 nozzle/tip and pipe 16 meringue kisses in slightly varying sizes onto the prepared baking sheet spaced evenly apart. Dust the tops of the meringues with a little matcha powder and bake in the preheated oven for around 30–40 minutes or until they easily lift from the baking sheet but are still soft in the centre.

To make the yuzu curd, combine the yuzu juice or purée, egg yolks, whole egg and sugar in a heatproof mixing bowl and whisk together. Set the bowl over a saucepan one-third of the way full with just simmering water. Make sure the base of the bowl does not touch the water. Continue to whisk over medium heat until the mixture starts to thicken. Remove from the heat and whisk for 1 minute more. Whisk in the diced butter, allow the curd to cool slightly and add a little lemon juice to taste. Cover the bowl with clingfilm/plastic wrap and chill in the fridge until needed.

To make the white chocolate cream, put the whipping/heavy cream in a small saucepan over high heat until just boiling. Remove from the heat and whisk in the white chocolate. Allow the mixture to cool then whisk in the double/heavy cream and set aside ready to construct the desserts.

To construct the desserts, transfer the yuzu curd to the piping/pastry bag with the size 4 nozzle. On your chosen serving plates, pipe a little yuzu curd and spread into a curve with a small palette knife/metal spatula. Make three quenelles of white chocolate cream (following the instructions on page 23) and arrange along the curve. Arrange four matcha meringues and sansho strawberries around the quenelles. Decorate with more piped dots of yuzu curd and sprigs of shiso cress for an extra punch of colour, if desired.

COMPRESSED WATERMELON & CHARRED GRAPEFRUIT SASHIMI WITH LIMONCELLO

This compressed fruit sashimi dish is inspired by the Japanese delicacy. I have chosen watermelon, grapefruit and raspberries but feel free to use whichever fruit you fancy, though I have to say I love this flavour combination. I use a vac pac machine to make my compressed fruit the day before I plan to serve, which gives an intense flavour, but you can marinate the fruit to impart flavour instead.

FRUIT GRATIN
sugar syrup: 2 parts water
   to 1 part caster/granulated
   sugar
1 star anise, grated
¼ watermelon
2 pink grapefruit
225-g/8-oz. punnet of fresh
   raspberries

SABAYON
4 egg yolks
80 g/⅓ cup plus 1 tablespoon
   caster/granulated sugar
175 g/¾ cup double/heavy
   cream, very lightly whipped
30 ml/2 tablespoons
   limoncello

TO SERVE (OPTIONAL)
shortbread biscuits
tahini ice cream

vac pack machine (optional)
cook's blowtorch
stand mixer with a whisk
   attachment
sugar thermometer
piping/pastry bag with a plain
   nozzle/tip (optional)

MAKES 4 DESSERTS

Make the fruit gratin the day before you plan to serve. Make up a small amount of a basic sugar syrup by heating together 2 parts water to 1 part sugar over low heat until the sugar has dissolved. Let cool a little. Add 1 tablespoon of the sugar syrup to a vac pac bag with the grated star anise.

Peel the watermelon and cut away most of the seeded area. Chop the flesh into chunks and remove any remaining seeds. Add to the vac pac bag and seal on full vacuum; you will see the fruit instantly change colour.

Alternatively, if you don't have a vac pac machine, you can marinate the watermelon chunks in the hot sugar syrup for 20 minutes instead.

The next day, peel the grapefruit and carefully cut the segments out by slicing into the fillets at the side of the pith in each segment. Lay these out about one finger-width apart on a baking sheet and allow to dry uncovered at room temperature for 2 hours. Once dry, use the cook's blow torch to create tiger print-style charring on the grapefruit. Set aside

To make the sabayon, put the egg yolks in the bowl of a stand mixer with the whisk attachment and start to beat at full speed. Meanwhile, put the sugar into a saucepan and add a little water to make a wet sand consistency. Add the sugar thermometer to the pan, set over medium heat and bring to the boil. When the temperature reaches 118°C (244°F) and the eggs are frothy, turn the speed on the mixer down to low and carefully pour the syrup down the side of the bowl, being careful not to get any on the whisks. Once combined, whisk the sabayon at high speed until cool; about 5 minutes. Fold in the lightly whipped cream followed by the limoncello. Transfer to a piping/pastry bag, if using, for finishing the dessert.

To construct the dessert, depending on your preference, you can slice the charred grapefruit very thinly (sashimi-style) or into slightly larger bite-sized pieces; I have opted for a combination of both. Divide the slices of compressed watermelon between each serving dish, and lay them out in a star shape, touching in the middle and alternating with slices of charred grapefruit. Arrange some raspberries over each plate to decorate. Pipe or spoon over the sabayon to cover and gratinate with the cook's blow torch. Serve immediately with shortbread biscuits and tahini ice cream, if you wish.

WHOLE YUZU CAKE WITH CRÈME FRAÎCHE, BASIL & OLIVE OIL POWDER

You can make these delicate cakes to serve as individually portioned desserts or as a large cake to serve with coffee. The olive oil powder may seem like an odd addition but it gives a light perfumed richness to the dessert. Delicious eaten warm or cold.

WHOLE YUZU CAKE
3 whole fresh yuzu fruits
4 UK large/US extra-large
    eggs
175 g/¾ cup plus
    2 tablespoons caster/
    granulated sugar
175 g/1¾ cups ground
    almonds
¼ teaspoon baking powder

OLIVE OIL POWDER
approx. 50 g/1¾ oz.
    maltodextrin powder
    (available online)
1 tablespoon good quality
    extra virgin olive oil

YUZU SYRUP
200 ml/generous ¾ cup
    yuzu juice
seeds from 1 vanilla pod/
    bean
100 g/½ cup caster/
    granulated sugar

TO DECORATE
300 ml/1¼ cups crème
    fraiche (or sour cream)
Greek basil (optional)

*12 x 6-cm/2-inch individual
    well-greased cake pans or
    silicone moulds or 1 large
    20-cm/8-inch greased and
    lined cake pan or mould
    piping/pastry bags (optional)*

MAKES 12 INDIVIDUAL
DESSERTS OR 1 LARGE
CAKE

To make the whole yuzu cake, put the yuzu fruits in a large saucepan, cover with water and boil for at least 1 hour with the lid on. Check the water and top up as necessary to make sure the fruit stay fully submerged.

When the fruit are soft and cooked all the way through to the centre, remove from the water and cut each in half. Reserve around 100 ml/⅓ cup of the cooking water. Check thoroughly inside the fruit for pips/seeds and remove any you find. Blitz the fruits in a food processor to make a smooth purée, adding the cooking water only if required. Set the purée aside to cool while you make the rest of the cake.

Preheat the oven to 180°C (350° F) Gas 4.

In the bowl of a stand mixer with the whisk attachment (or using a hand-held electric whisk), cream the eggs and sugar together until light and fluffy. In a separate bowl mix together the ground almonds and baking powder, then carefully fold into the egg and sugar mixture. Fold in the cooled yuzu purée until fully combined. Pipe or spoon the cake mixture into the individual moulds or the large mould and bake in the preheated oven for 12 minutes for individual cakes or 45–50 minutes for a large cake. A skewer inserted into the centre should come out clean. The cakes might sink slightly when removed from the oven but that is fine. Carefully turn the cakes out of their moulds (or large mould) and leave to cool on a wire rack.

To make the olive oil powder, gradually whisk the maltodextrin powder into the olive oil until the mixture has the texture of a powder. Add a little more maltodextrin until you get the right texture. Set aside ready for plating.

To make the yuzu syrup, combine the yuzu juice, vanilla seeds and sugar in a saucepan and set over high heat. Boil until the mixture has thickened enough to coat the back of a spoon. Remove the syrup from the heat, allow it to cool and set aside for plating.

To construct the desserts, remove the cakes from their moulds and put on a serving plate. Spread the top of each with a neat layer of yuzu syrup. Pipe a crown of crème fraiche around the top edge of each cake. Decorate in the same way if you have made the larger cake and cut into slices. Decorate the serving plates with some more yuzu syrup and sprinkle over the olive oil powder. Add a few sprigs of Greek basil to garnish, if you like.

BITTER CHOCOLATE FONDANT, MISO BANANA PARFAIT & HIBIKI WHISKY ICE CREAM

This recipe was a favourite of mine in my days as Head Pastry Chef at the Mandarin Oriental Hotel in London. I would advise you to make everything apart from the fondants the day before, as they take several hours but will keep well.

BANANA CRISPS
100 g/½ cup caster/
    granulated sugar
2–3 bananas, not too green
    but not overly ripe
freshly squeezed juice
    of 1 lemon

HIBIKI WHISKY ICE CREAM
100 g/3½ oz. egg yolks
    (approx. 5 medium)
25 g/1¼ tablespoons liquid
    glucose
135 g/generous ⅔ cup
    caster/granulated sugar
250 ml/generous 1 cup
    whole milk
250 ml/1 cup crème fraîche
70 ml/⅓ cup Hibiki whisky
    (if unavailable, a good
    single malt whisky will do)

MISO BANANA PARFAIT
100 g/½ cup caster/
    granulated sugar
1 tablespoon sweet miso
    paste
leftover banana from
    your banana crisps
50 ml/3½ tablespoons
    crème de banane
80 g/2¾ oz. egg yolks
125 g/scant ⅔ cup caster/
    granulated sugar
40 g/2 tablespoons liquid
    glucose

continued overleaf

To make the banana crisps, preheat the oven to 100°C (215°F) Gas ¼. Or use the warming drawer in your oven if you have one. Put the sugar in a saucepan with 100 ml/generous ⅓ cup water and boil until the sugar has completely dissolved. Set aside to cool.

Slice the bananas lengthways very carefully using a mandoline or a long sharp knife. Try to get whole very thin slices the length of the banana. This may take practise – hence the allowance of two–three bananas to get the eight crisps you need. Reserve leftover scraps for the parfait.

Put the eight best banana slices on a silicone mat and brush them with lemon juice on one side. Leave in the warming drawer or preheated low oven for around 1 hour until dry to the touch but not too coloured (if the bananas curl it means they were too ripe).

Once completely dry, increase or set the oven temperature to 180°C (350°F) Gas 4. Brush the bananas with the cooled sugar syrup, then return to the oven and bake for around 10 minutes until golden. Remove from the oven and straight away (being careful not to burn yourself) mould the bananas into curved tuile shapes around a small, thin rolling pin or the handle of a whisk (see **A**, overleaf). Set aside ready for plating or store at room temperature in an airtight container if making the night before.

To make the ice cream, whisk together the egg yolks, liquid glucose and sugar in a large bowl and set aside. Put the milk in a saucepan and heat over medium heat until just boiling. Slowly pour the hot milk into the egg and sugar mixture, whisking to combine. Return the mixture to a saucepan over low heat and cook, stirring with a wooden spoon, until the custard is thick enough to coat the back of the spoon, or until it reaches 78°C (172°F). Decant into a bowl and cool over ice, stirring occasionally. When cool, whisk in the crème fraîche and the whisky to taste. It should be fairly boozy to stand up to the other punchy flavours in the dessert. Transfer to an ice cream machine and churn to the desired consistency. Freeze until required.

To make the miso banana parfait, first make a banana purée. Put the 100 g/½ cup of sugar, miso paste and the leftover banana scraps from the banana crisps into a preheated saucepan. Cook for 5 minutes over medium heat, stirring, until the banana begins to break down. Stir in the crème de banane, reserving a little. At this point you can blitz the purée in a blender if you want a really smooth-texture, but I like it as it is. Set aside to cool.

A

B

C

D

500 ml/generous 2 cups whipping/heavy cream, semi-whipped

readymade cake sponge sheets or sliced banana cake for the base OR tempered sheets of dark/bittersweet chocolate cut to the same size as your pan (optional)

BITTER CHOCOLATE FONDANTS
4 eggs
150 g/¾ cup caster/granulated sugar
100 g/3½ oz. dark/bittersweet chocolate, melted
85 g/¾ stick butter, melted
25 g/3 tablespoons plain/all-purpose flour
icing/confectioners' sugar or cocoa powder, for dusting
sheet of tempered chocolate, to make decorations

mandoline (optional)
silicone mat
ice cream machine
stand mixer with a whisk attachment
sugar thermometer
12 x 6-cm/4½ x 2½-inch baking pan, for the parfait
8-cm/3-inch metal cake moulds, for the fondants, greased with oil spray
piping/pastry bag with a large plain nozzle/tip

MAKES 8 DESSERTS

Next, put the egg yolks into the bowl of a stand mixer with the whisk attachment and begin to beat at medium speed. Meanwhile, stir together the 125 g/scant ⅔ cup caster/granulated sugar with the liquid glucose and a little water to make a wet sand consistency. Add the sugar thermometer and make sure the edge of the saucepan is completely clean. Set over high heat and take the temperature up to 118°C (244°F). When the temperature has been reached and the egg yolks are frothy, slowly pour the hot syrup down the side of the bowl into the egg yolks, whisking at low speed and being careful not to get any syrup onto the whisks. Once all the syrup is incorporated, increase the speed and whisk for 10–15 minutes until the mixture doubles in volume. Reduce the speed and whisk until the mixture is cool. Fold in the banana purée followed by the semi-whipped cream. Taste and add a little extra crème de banane if required.

If you would like a base and top to your parfait, cut thin slices of cake and put in the base of the prepared baking pan. Or use a sheet of tempered dark/bittersweet chocolate cut to size. Alternatively, you can have the parfait as it is. Pour the parfait into the baking pan, level out with a palette knife/metal spatula and add another sheet of cake or chocolate on top, if using. Freeze for at least 6 hours. Once completely frozen, use a sharp knife dipped in hot water to cut the parfait into eight 6 x 3-cm/2¼ x 1¼ inch rectangles and return to the freezer until needed.

To make the bitter chocolate fondants, put the cake moulds on a large baking sheet on top of a square each of non-stick baking parchment. Line them carefully with a cylinder of non-stick baking parchment **(B)**.

Peheat the oven to 180°C (350°F) Gas 4.

Use a hand-held electric whisk to beat together the eggs and sugar until the whisks leave a ribbon-like trail in the mixture. Fold in the melted chocolate and then the melted butter. Firmly fold in the flour until fully incorporated. Transfer the mixture to the fridge for 1 hour to rest.

Have all the other dessert elements ready for plating as you want to serve the fondants immediately after cooking. Put the chilled mixture into a piping/pastry bag and pipe to fill two-thirds of the way up the prepared moulds. Bake the fondants in the preheated oven for 8–10 minutes.

To construct the desserts, dust the fondants with cocoa powder or icing/confectioners' sugar while still in their rings, then use a fish slice to carefully transfer to the serving plates. Remove the metal ring and baking parchment from the fondants and peel off the paper from the outside of the cakes **(C)**. Add a slice of banana parfait on the other side of each plate and top with a neat quenelle (see page 23) of whisky ice cream and a banana crisp. Cut a sheet of temepred chocolate into very thin strips **(D)** to make an additional decoration, if desired.

COOKIES & CONFECTIONERY

HAVE A LITTLE FUN WITH THIS CHAPTER FULL OF PLAYFUL, SLIGHTLY NOSTALGIC RECIPES. START WITH MY SIMPLE BUT ENTIRELY ELEGANT SESAME PEANUT COOKIES OR CARAMELIZED SWEET MISO TRUFFLES. MASTER THE MACARON AND FINISH WITH THE SLIGHTLY MORE ADVANCED MATCHA 'KIT KAT' OR SUDACHI, YUZU & MIKAN FRUIT LOLLIPOPS WITH YOGURT SHERBET DIP.

SWEET MISO, SATO NISHIKI CHERRY & YUZU FRUIT MACARONS

If you follow this recipe carefully you should achieve top pâtisserie-standard macarons every time. Mix and match colours and flavours to your preference.

MACARON SHELLS

275 g/1½ cups minus
  2 tablespoons caster/
  superfine sugar
95 g/3¼ oz. egg whites
  (approx. 3 egg whites)
275 g/2¾ cups ground
  almonds
275 g/2 cups icing/
  confectioners' sugar
95 g/3¼ oz. egg whites
  (approx. 3 egg whites)
½ teaspoon professional-
  grade pink food colouring
½ teaspoon professional-
  grade yellow food
  colouring
½ teaspoon professional-
  grade purple food
  colouring

YUZU FILLING

75 g/⅓ cup yuzu juice
  or purée
2 egg yolks
1 egg
50 g/¼ cup caster/superfine
  sugar
50 g/3½ tablespoons butter,
  diced
a small squeeze of fresh
  lemon juice, to taste

continued overleaf

To make the macaron shells, combine the caster/superfine sugar with 100 ml/⅓ cup plus 1 tablespoon of water in a small saucepan and mix until fully dissolved. Set the saucepan over medium-high heat with the sugar thermometer inside. While the syrup is heating, ready the first 95 g/3¼ oz. of egg whites in the bowl of a stand mixer with the whisk attachment.

When the temperature on the sugar thermometer reaches 110°C (230°F), turn the mixer on and begin beating the egg whites at a medium speed. When the temperature reaches 114°C (237°F) and the egg whites have become frothy, lift the thermometer out and slowly and carefully pour the hot syrup down the side of the bowl (see **A**, overleaf) being careful not to get any hot syrup on the whisks. Increase the mixing speed to maximum and continue to whip for approximately 5 minutes or until the Italian meringue mixture looks glossy and soft peaks have formed.

While the Italian meringue is whisking, make the paste. In a separate clean mixing bowl, combine the ground almonds with the icing/confectioners' sugar and add the other 95 g/3¼ oz. egg whites. Mix with a wooden spoon until fully incorporated and you have a stiff paste. When the Italian meringue is at soft peak stage switch off the mixer. You are now ready to combine the Italian meringue with the paste in three careful stages (if it is over-mixed, it will become too liquid and the macarons will not rise). Add one-third of the meringue to the paste and mix in firmly and quickly using a wooden spoon or spatula to ensure there are no lumps (see **B**, overleaf). Fold in a second third of the meringue mixture more gently. Add the final third of the meringue mixture very gently indeed and fold until just incorporated (see **C**, overleaf). Split the entire mixture into three equal portions in three clean bowls. Add the pink food colouring to one, yellow food colouring to the next and purple food colouring to the third. Again, fold in very gently until just incorporated.

Preheat the oven to 145°C (300°F) Gas 2.

Using a spatula, fill a piping/pastry bag half-full with each of the three mixtures. Taking the pink first, pipe some mix onto each corner of the baking sheets to stick the baking parchment lining firmly down (see **D**, overleaf). Pipe around 20 even circles of mixture in straight lines leaving a 2-cm/¾ inch gap between each (see **E**, overleaf). You can use a pre-drawn stencil to guide you if you wish, the macarons should be about 4 cm/1½ inches in diameter. Repeat the process for the other two colours on the two separate baking

SATO NISHIKI CHERRY FILLING

120 g/generous ½ cup Sato Nishiki cherry purée

2 egg yolks

45 g/3½ tablespoons caster/superfine sugar

200 g/1¾ sticks butter, diced

MISO FILLING

80 ml/⅓ cup whipping/heavy cream

20 g/1 tablespoon liquid glucose

100 g/½ cup caster/superfine sugar

a pinch of sea salt

30 g/2 level tablespoons sweet miso paste

sugar thermometer

stand mixer with a whisk attachment

6 piping/pastry bags fitted with large plain nozzles/tips

3 baking sheets, lined with non-stick baking parchment

MAKES APPROX. 30 MACARONS (10 IN EACH FLAVOUR)

sheets. Tap the baking sheets down on the work surface to get rid of any traces left from the piping process. Bake the first batch in the preheated oven for around 17–19 minutes or until the macaron shells are risen and lift easily from the baking sheet. Leave the macaron shells to cool and repeat for the other two batches.

To make the yuzu fruit filling, whisk together the yuzu juice or purée, egg yolks, whole egg and caster/superfine sugar in a heatproof mixing bowl. Set the mixing bowl over a saucepan of just simmering water ensuring the base of the bowl does not touch the water. Continue to whisk over a medium heat until the mixture starts to thicken; this should happen fairly quickly. Remove the bowl from the heat and whisk for 1 minute more, then beat in the diced butter. Allow the mixture to cool slightly and add a little lemon juice to taste. Scrape into a piping/pastry bag and refrigerate until needed.

To make the Sato Nishiki cherry filling, warm the Sato Nishiki purée in a small saucepan set over medium heat. In a separate bowl, whisk together the egg yolks and caster/superfine sugar. When the Sato Nishiki purée begins to boil, add a little to the egg mixture and whisk to combine. Transfer this back into the saucepan with the rest of the boiled cherries and stir with a spatula over low heat until the mixture is thick enough to coat the back of the spatula or until the temperature reaches 80°C (176°F). Pour into the clean bowl of your stand mixer with the whisk attachment and beat at medium speed for 2 minutes. After 2 minutes, add the diced butter piece by piece. Continue to whisk for a further 2 minutes or until you have a thick, smooth and shiny filling. Using a spatula, scrape the mixture into a piping/pastry bag and set aside in the fridge until needed.

To make the miso filling, put the whipping/heavy cream into a microwaveable bowl and warm gently for 30 seconds. Put the liquid glucose and caster/superfine sugar in a saucepan over a medium heat and stir constantly until you get a rich, dark caramel. Remove the pan from the heat and gradually add the warm cream, still stirring constantly. Be very careful as the caramel will froth up. Once all the cream has been incorporated stir in the sea salt and sweet miso paste. Allow the filling to cool, then use a spatula to scrape into a piping/pastry bag and refrigerate until needed.

To construct the macarons, arrange the shells in columns and match tops and bottoms with similarly sized and coloured other halves. On alternate columns, pipe the yuzu filling on the yellow halves, Sato Nishiki cherry filling on the pink halves and miso filling on the purple halves (F). Sandwich the macarons together with the other half of their matching shell and leave to set before serving.

MATCHA ALFAJORES

This is a simple yet delicious recipe for a traditional South American sandwich cookie – with a couple of Japanese twists. It is such a delicately textured treat and a delightful option for part of an afternoon tea or just to have with a cup of coffee. I have used a sweet miso caramel to replace the traditional dulce de leche filling.

ALFAJORES
200 g/1½ cups plain/
   all-purpose flour
325 g/1¼ cups cornflour/
   cornstarch
½ teaspoon bicarbonate
   of soda/baking soda
2 teaspoons baking powder
150 g/¾ cup caster/
   granulated sugar
225 g/2 sticks butter,
   softened
3 egg yolks
10 g/2 level tablespoons
   matcha powder

MISO CARAMEL
160 ml/generous ¾ cup
   whipping/heavy cream
40 g/2 tablespoons liquid
   glucose
200 g/1 cup caster/superfine
   sugar
1 level teaspoon sea salt
60 g/3 level tablespoons
   sweet miso paste
icing/confectioners' sugar,
   for dusting

*3-cm/1-inch round cookie
   cutter
2 baking sheets, lined with
   non-stick baking parchment
piping/pastry bag with a plain
   nozzle/tip (optional)*

MAKES 16 COOKIES

To make the alfajores, mix together the flour, cornflour/cornstarch, bicarbonate of soda/baking soda and baking powder; set aside.

Beat the sugar with the softened butter at medium speed in the bowl of a stand mixer with the whisk attachment (or using a hand-held electric whisk) until light and fluffy. Add the egg yolks one at a time, allowing each to fully incorporate into the butter mixture before adding the next. Lastly, add the matcha powder and beat until fully combined.

Gently fold in the flour mixture to form a crumbly dough – you may need to add a little water to bring together. When the dough becomes cohesive enough, press it together into a ball with your hands and wrap in clingfilm/plastic wrap. Refrigerate for at least 30 and up to 60 minutes.

Preheat the oven to 180°C (350°F) Gas 4.

Roll out the dough, using as little flour as possible on the work surface, to a thickness of around 6 mm/¼ inch. Stamp out rounds with the cookie cutter. Continue pressing the dough together, rolling it out, and cutting until you have used it all – you should be able to make 32 halves for the 16 cookies. Arrange the cookies evenly spaced apart on the prepared baking sheets. Bake in the preheated oven for around 7–10 minutes until set but not browned. Remove the cookies from the oven and leave to cool on a wire rack.

To make the miso caramel, place the whipping/heavy cream into a microwaveable bowl and warm gently for 30 seconds. Put the liquid glucose and sugar in a small saucepan and heat gently, stirring constantly until a rich dark caramel is achieved. Remove the pan from the heat and carefully add the warm cream, stirring constantly. Be very careful as the caramel will froth up so add the cream gradually. Once all the cream has been incorporated, stir in the salt and miso paste. Allow the caramel to cool and then scrape into a piping/pastry bag, if using, ready for filling the alfajores.

To construct the cookies, match up the cookie halves with those of a similar size and colour and pipe or spoon a generous bulb of miso caramel into the middle of half the cookies. Sandwich the other halves on top and dust the tops of the cookies with icing/confectioners' sugar. These will keep nicely for about a week stored in an airtight container.

MATCHA 'KIT KAT'

The green tea Kit Kat is the Japanese twist on the popular chocolate bar, adored by kids and adults alike. I have had a go at making my own version of this famous treat. The secret to the layers in a real Kit Kat is to use the wafer offcuts to create an extra-light texture, so I have done the same here. I use Valrhona Dulcey chocolate, which gives a unique, rich flavour to balance out the earthiness of the matcha.

WAFER
160 g/5⅔ oz. egg whites
80 g/⅓ cup plus 1 tablespoon
  caster/granulated sugar
160 g/1⅓ cups sifted icing/
  confectioners' sugar
160 g/generous 1½ cups
  ground almonds

FILLING
approx. 100 g/1¾–2 cups
  leftover wafer trimmings
  (from recipe above)
150 g/5¼ oz. Valrhona
  Dulcey chocolate

MATCHA MOUSSE
6 egg yolks
125 g/⅔ cup minus
  2 teaspoons caster/
  granulated sugar
4 large sheets or 8 small
  domestic leaves of gelatine,
  soaked in cold water
10 g/2 level tablespoons
  matcha powder
200 g/7 oz. Valrhona Dulcey
  chocolate
350 g/generous 1½ cups
  whipping/heavy cream,
  semi-whipped

Preheat the oven to 180°C (350°F) Gas 4.

To make the wafer, put the egg whites in the bowl of a stand mixer with the whisk attachment and beat to soft peaks. Increase the mixing speed and slowly add the sugar, beating until glossy with stiff peaks. Fold in the icing/confectioners' sugar followed by the ground almonds. Spread the mixture onto the prepared baking sheet and bake in the preheated oven for around 15–20 minutes; it should be pale and still a little soft in the middle.

Remove from the oven (leaving the oven on) and invert the paper onto another clean sheet of non-stick baking parchment. Remove the top layer of parchment and use a large sharp knife to cut the wafer into 12 strips (6 × 1 cm/2¾ × ⅜ inch) and reserve the offcuts. Place the strips and offcuts (still on the parchment) back on the baking sheet in the hot oven. Bake for about another 5 minutes until golden brown. Keep a close eye on it as the wafer will colour quickly. Set aside to cool.

To make filling, crush the wafer offcuts to small pieces. Melt the Valrhona Dulcey chocolate in a heatproof bowl set over a pan of barely simmering water. Make sure that the base of the bowl does not touch the water. Mix the melted chocolate and crushed wafer together until well combined. Use a rolling pin to roll out the mixture as evenly as possible between two sheets of non-stick baking parchment until very thin. Freeze the mixture (still in the paper) until completely set; around 30 minutes.

Once set, cut out four pieces the exact size of your silicone moulds; these will be the bases. Set aside in the freezer. Next cut out eight pieces the size of the wafers made earlier (6 × 1 cm/2¾ × ⅜ inch).

Divide the 12 wafers into four lots of three and the eight pieces of filling into four lots of two. Sandwich together three pieces of wafer with two pieces of filling in alternating layers. Repeat for the remaining Kit Kats. Wrap each stack in clingfilm/plastic wrap and set aside in the freezer until needed.

To make the matcha mousse, whisk the egg yolks at high speed in a stand mixer until foamy. Meanwhile, put the sugar into a saucepan with enough water to make a wet sand consistency. Add the sugar thermometer and set over medium heat. When the temperature of the syrup reaches 118°C (244°F) and the egg yolks are frothy, turn the mixer down to slow and carefully pour the syrup down the side of the bowl, being careful not

continued overleaf

GREEN CHOCOLATE SPRAY

a store-bought green velvet aerosol spray (see suppliers page 176)

OR if you have a pâtisserie food-grade spray gun:

200 g/7 oz. cocoa butter

300 g/10½ oz. white chocolate

approx. 30 g/1 oz. green cocoa fat colouring

silver leaf and tempered chocolate sticks, to decorate (optional)

stand mixer with a whisk attachment

baking sheet, lined with non-stick baking parchment

piping/pastry bag with a plain nozzle/tip

sugar thermometer

4 rectangular silicone moulds (see suppliers page 176)

MAKES 4

to get any hot syrup on the whisks. Squeeze the excess water from the soaked gelatine and add to the mixture. Mix on high for a further few minutes as the mixture cools. Add the matcha powder and mix until incorporated. Meanwhile, melt the chocolate in a heatproof bowl set over a pan of barely simmering water. Make sure the base of the bowl does not touch the water. Fold the melted chocolate into the mousse, followed by the semi-whipped cream. Transfer to a piping/pastry bag.

To construct the desserts, pipe a little matcha mousse into the moulds and spread with a palette knife/metal spatula into every nook and cranny. Tap the mould on the work surface to remove any air bubbles that may spoil the finish of the desserts. Pipe in more mousse to fill about half-way up and then insert the wafer tower inserts. Fill any gaps with more matcha mousse and scrape the tops level with a palette knife/metal spatula. Add the wafer bases and freeze the whole desserts for around 4 hours or until set.

To decorate, carefully remove the desserts from their moulds and transfer to a wire rack. Put down some paper to protect the work surface. If you are making the green chocolate spray, melt the cocoa butter and white chocolate together and add green colouring to your preferred shade. Transfer to the spray gun, and use straight away to spray the desserts all over. Or use store-bought green velvet aerosol spray. Let the coating set before serving. Decorate with some silver leaf and tempered chocolate sticks, as desired.

SESAME PEANUT COOKIES

These nutty shortbread-like cookies are truly delicious – the addition of sesame seeds works so well. This recipe was handed down to me by Lisa Phillips, an incredible Pastry Chef who I had the pleasure of working with at the Mandarin Oriental Hotel.

250 g/2¼ sticks butter

150 g/¾ cup caster/granulated sugar

140 g/⅔ cup light brown soft sugar

250 g/1¼ cups smooth peanut butter

400 g/3 cups plain/all-purpose flour

22 g/1½ tablespoons baking powder

1 tablespoon each crushed salted peanuts and white sesame seeds, mixed together for, sprinkling

2 baking sheets, lined with non-stick baking parchment

MAKES 20 COOKIES

Put the butter, caster/granulated sugar and light brown soft sugar in a mixing bowl and cream together using a hand-held electric whisk until light and fluffy. Add the peanut butter and stir with a wooden spoon until just incorporated. Sift in the flour and baking powder and mix until the dough comes together. It will have a crumbly, short texture.

Roll out the dough between two sheets of non-stick baking parchment to roughly the size of the baking sheet. Remove the top sheet of paper and lightly sprinkle the dough with the mixture of crushed peanuts and white sesame seeds. Transfer the dough to the freezer between the two sheets of non-stick baking parchment to firm up – this will make it easier to cut.

Preheat the oven to 170°C (350) Gas 4.

Use a sharp knife and a ruler to cut the chilled dough into 7 cm/2¾ inch squares; any excess dough can be mixed together and rolled out again.

Place the cookies on the prepared baking sheets and bake in the preheated oven for 8–13 minutes until golden. Leave to cool on a wire rack.

pictured page 144

PEANUT AMANATTŌ

A traditional Japanese confectionery, amanattō is usually made with beans such as soy or adzuki, which are candied in a sugar syrup. I've combined the beans with salted peanuts here to add a bit of crunch. They make for a moreish nibble to serve with drinks. You can add a little wasabi at the end of cooking for an interesting kick.

200 g/1¼ cups dried adzuki beans

200 g/1½ cups salted roasted peanuts

300 g/1½ cups caster/granulated sugar

50 g/¼ cup light brown soft sugar

SERVES 10

Soak the adzuki beans overnight in plenty of cold water. Drain and rinse well.

Put the beans in a large saucepan, cover with water and place over medium-high heat. Bring to the boil, then cover the pan and simmer for about an hour until soft; topping up the pan with more water as necessary so that the beans are always submerged. Cool the beans by draining under cold running water. Dry thoroughly on paper towels.

Put the peanuts, sugar and 3½ tablespoons water in a wide saucepan or deep frying pan/skillet. Set over medium heat and cook, stirring, for 5 minutes. Add the beans and cook until everything is coated in the sugar. Stir in the light brown soft sugar. Tip onto a tray to cool before serving.

pictured page 145

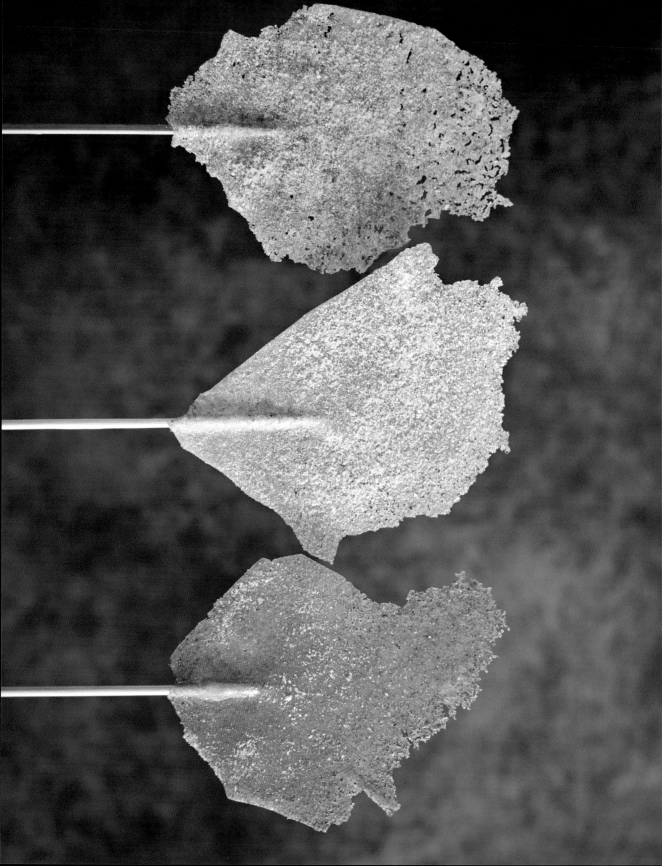

SUDACHI, YUZU & MIKAN FRUIT LOLLIPOPS WITH YOGURT SHERBET DIP

You will need to hunt down the fresh Japanese fruits to make these lollipops, alternatively, there are other citrus fruits you can use if they are too difficult to find. Consult the flavour wheel at the start of the book to make sure you use the right flavour profile. I have made rustic free-form lollies but you could use stencils if you want a more uniform shape.

LOLLIPOPS
zest of 1 sudachi fruit, 1 yuzu fruit and 1 mikan fruit
300 g/2 cups plus 2 tablespoons fondant icing/confectioners' sugar
200 g/⅔ cup liquid glucose
3 g/½ teaspoon citric acid, divided into three equal portions

YOGURT SHERBET DIP
200 g/1 cup acidic yogurt powder (available online)
200 g/1½ cups minus 1 tablespoon icing/confectioners' sugar

sugar thermometer
3 baking sheets, lined with non-stick baking parchment or a silicone mat
lollipop sticks
small tea strainer

MAKES 12 LOLLIPOPS

Place the zest of all three fruits separately on a heatproof tray and leave in a warm place to dry for 24 hours. Alternatively, place the tray with the zest in an oven on its lowest setting until completely dry; about 1½–2 hours.

Meanwhile, combine the fondant icing/confectioners' sugar with the liquid glucose in a small saucepan set over low heat. Put a sugar thermometer into the pan and slowly take the temperature up to 156°C (313°F). When the correct temperature has been reached, carefully pour the hot syrup onto the prepared baking sheet. Allow the sugar mixture to cool and set completely (about 1 hour), then break up the slab of sugar into small shards.

Weigh the shards into three equal portions. In three separate small bowls, put each of the three dried fruit zests and add to these a portion each of the sugar shards and a portion each of the citric acid. Blitz each mixture separately to a fine powder in a food processor or blender.

Preheat the oven to 180°C (350°F) Gas 4.

Use the small tea strainer to gently dust a layer of one of the lolly mixtures over a prepared baking sheet. Try to make sure the layer is as even as possible because too little means the lollipops will be too thin and brittle, too generous and it will be too thick and not delicate.

Bake the lollipop mixture in the preheated oven for 3–4 minutes or until melted. Remove the baking sheet from the oven and allow to cool and set again. Leave the oven on.

Break the set mixture into rustic shards and place a shard on top of each lolly stick back on the lined baking sheet, spaced evenly apart. Return to the hot oven for around 2 minutes until the mixture has melted over the sticks. Remove from the oven and carefully squeeze the lollipops around the sticks to ensure they adhere. Allow to cool and set firm before serving. Repeat for the other two lollipop mixtures.

To make the yogurt sherbet dip, mix the acidic yogurt powder with the icing/confectioners' sugar. Serve the lollipops with the dip on the side.

Note If you want to make your lollipops brightly coloured instead of the natural hues pictured, add a couple of drops of food colouring to the syrup.

HOT SAKE JELLY SHOTS WITH GINGER SPHERIFICATION

These jelly shots are certainly a conversation starter. The spherification technique always looks impressive and can be used to decorate many desserts. It sounds scientific but actually the process is quite straightforward. The key thing to remember is that spherification needs to be served within 15 minutes of being made.

SAKE JELLY
500 ml/2 cups plus
   2 tablespoons sake
3 g gellan gum mixed with
10 g/2½ teaspoons caster/
   granulated sugar to
   disperse

GINGER SYRUP
150 g/¾ cup caster/
   granulated sugar
5-cm/2-inch thumb of fresh
   ginger, peeled and finely
   chopped

SPHERIFICATION
250 ml/1 cup plus
   1 tablespoon ginger syrup
   (above)
10 g/2½ teaspoons caster/
   granulated sugar
use a readymade kit
   (see suppliers page 176)
   or: 2.5 g/½ teaspoon
   sodium alginate
5 g/1 teaspoon calcium
   chloride

*heatproof shot glasses
scales that can measure
   in small increments,
   for the gellan gum*

MAKES 10 DESSERTS

To make the hot sake jelly, put 100 ml/generous ⅓ cup of the sake in a saucepan and bring to the boil. Remove the pan from the heat, then whisk in the gellan gum and sugar mixture. Whisking constantly, bring back to the boil until dissolved. Remove from the heat and whisk in the remaining sake. Transfer to a jug/pitcher and divide between the shot glasses. Let cool a little, then refrigerate for 30 minutes to set.

To make the ginger syrup, put the sugar in a saucepan with 300 ml/generous 1¼ cups water over medium heat. Bring the syrup to the boil and ensure all the sugar has dissolved. Stir through the chopped fresh ginger, then remove from the heat and allow to infuse for 20 minutes. Strain the ginger syrup through a fine-mesh sieve/strainer, discarding the lumps of ginger. Set the ginger syrup aside to cool a little – this will be used to make the spherification.

To make the spherification, follow the steps on page 24. Get everything ready to go and make the spherification at the last minute before you serve.

To construct the desserts, warm the shot glasses with the jelly in the microwave for 30–60 seconds. Use a spoon to delicately top each jelly with the ginger spherification. Serve the desserts immediately with a teaspoon.

CRISPY HIJIKI CHOCOLATE SEAWEED WITH PONZU DIPPING SAUCE

This is a very simple recipe and it works beautifully as an interactive party snack. The crispy, salty fried seaweed is dusted with sugar and cocoa powder and the idea is that your guests can use chopsticks to dip it into the spicy ponzu dip. To save time, it is perfectly acceptable to buy a good-quality ready-made ponzu sauce from a Japanese supermarket or online (see suppliers page 176).

50-g/1¾-oz. pack dried
  hijiki seaweed
100 g/½ cup caster/
  granulated sugar,
  for sprinkling
50 g/½ cup cocoa powder,
  for sprinkling

PONZU DIPPING SAUCE
2 tablespoons dark soy sauce
1 tablespoon bonito flakes
2 teaspoons Japanese rice
  vinegar
1 teaspoon mirin
1 tablespoon yuzu juice
  or purée

*deep-fat fryer or large
  wok filled half-full
  with vegetable oil*

SERVES 4

To make the crispy hijiki seaweed, preheat the vegetable oil in a deep-fat fryer until the temperature reaches 180°C (350°F). Or fill a large wok half-full with vegetable oil and heat until a cube of bread sizzles and rises to the surface instantly. Remove the seaweed from the packaging and fry in the hot oil for approximately 15 seconds. Take care as the oil can spit a lot during frying. Remove the seaweed with a slotted spoon and drain on paper towels. Set aside.

To make the ponzu dipping sauce, put all the ingredients apart from the yuzu juice or purée in a saucepan. Set over low-medium heat and simmer for around 5 minutes. Do not let the mixture boil. Strain through a fine-mesh sieve/strainer and then stir in the yuzu juice or purée. Let cool before serving.

To construct the snack, gently toss the fried seaweed with the sugar and cocoa powder and serve with the ponzu dip on the side.

CARAMELIZED SWEET MISO TRUFFLES

These decadent little beauties are easy to whip up and can be made well in advance and frozen. Alternatively, they will keep nicely in the fridge for up to a week.

INNER TRUFFLE
50 g/¼ cup caster/granulated sugar
200 g/⅔ cup sweet miso paste
200 ml/generous ¾ cup whipping/heavy cream
500 g/17 oz. dark/bittersweet chocolate, chopped
400 g/14 oz. milk/semisweet chocolate, chopped
60 g/½ stick butter, diced

OUTER TRUFFLE
100 g/3½ oz. dark/ bittersweet chocolate
50 g/½ cup cocoa powder

baking sheet, lined with non-stick baking parchment
baking sheet, lined with clingfilm/plastic wrap

MAKES ABOUT
20 TRUFFLES

Put the sugar into a saucepan and set over medium heat. As the sugar starts to melt and caramelize, whisk in the miso paste followed by the whipping/heavy cream. Bring the mixture to the boil, then remove the pan from the heat and add the dark/bittersweet and milk/semisweet chocolate. Allow the chocolate to melt, then add the diced butter and stir occasionally until melted. Pour the truffle mixture into a container and place in the fridge for 1 hour to set.

Once completely set, use a spoon or a melon baller to scoop out rough little balls of around 8–10 cm/3–4 inches in diameter; don't worry about the shape too much at this stage as you can neaten them later. Transfer the chocolates to the first prepared baking sheet lined with baking parchment and put into the freezer to set firm again; about another hour.

Once firm, roll the chocolates between the palms of your hands to shape into individual inner truffles – they do not need to be perfectly round. Put them back in the freezer for 1 hour to firm up, ready for dipping.

Melt half of the dark/bittersweet chocolate by blasting quickly in the microwave for around 30–60 seconds, then beat in the remaining chocolate until melted. Prepare the cocoa powder in a shallow dish or plate.

Put about a teaspoon of the melted chocolate in the palm of your hand and roll a truffle between your palms to give a delicate, even coating. Deposit into the cocoa powder and roll to give a generous coating. Transfer the truffles to the second prepared baking sheet lined with clingfilm/plastic wrap as you finish each one and return the full batch back to the fridge until the chocolate coating has set.

SAVOURIES

INSPIRED BY TRIPS TO THE BUSTLING STREET-FOOD
MARKETS OF JAPAN, MY SLIGHTLY REFINED VERSIONS
OF THESE SAVOURY TREATS ARE PACKED FULL OF
AUTHENTIC FLAVOURS. SIMPLE TO PREPARE, THEY
MAKE THE PERFECT ACCOMPANIMENT TO ANY OF THE
SWEET TREATS IN THIS BOOK. I HOPE YOU ENJOY THEM.

FURIKAKE POPCORN

Furikake is traditionally used in Japan as a seasoning to be sprinkled over cooked rice, considered almost as essential as salt and pepper. The core ingredients usually consist of sesame seeds, ground seaweed, sugar and salt but it does also come in a variety of flavours. Sometimes extra nori, crushed bonito flakes or wasabi are added. For ease, I would recommend you buy a ready-made seasoning online or from a specialist Japanese store, but you can simply mix together equal quantities of the core ingredients if you would rather. I have chosen the furikake with added wasabi, the overall flavour it gives the popcorn is wonderfully complex compared to standard store-bought popcorn. An easy way of surprising your guests with unusual, tasty flavours – it makes a great snack or even precursor to a Japanese meal.

1½ tablespoons sunflower oil (or any other high-heat tolerant oil such as vegetable or rapeseed oil)
200 g/1 cup unpopped popcorn kernels
50 ml/3½ tablespoons sesame oil
2–3 tablespoons store-bought wasabi furikake seasoning

MAKES 1 LARGE BOWL

Put the sunflower oil into a large saucepan with a lid. Add the corn kernels and mix to give an even coating of the oil. Place the lid on top and set the pan over low-medium heat, be careful it does not get too hot or the popcorn may burn.

Listen for the sound of popping and once the popping starts to slow the popcorn will be almost ready. Turn off the heat at this point and wait for the popping noise to stop completely.

Remove the pan from the stove and add the sesame oil and furikake seasoning. Stir through and serve.

VARIATION
You can make hundreds of variations on this simple recipe if you can't find furikake. Try replacing the oil with butter and the furikake with wasabi powder, a little sugar and some sesame seeds.

GYOZA CHICKEN WINGS KARAAGE-STYLE

A favourite bar snack served all over Japan, these moreish deep-fried stuffed chicken wings are often found in traditional izakaya establishments, the equivalent of British gastro pubs or traditional American taverns. They are a fantastic way to use up a cheap and often forgotten part of the chicken and make a stunning canapé or appetizer to serve at any occasion. You can change the filling and stuff these with minced shrimp or finely chopped mixed mushrooms and Asian vegetables, if you like.

20 chicken wings, deboned, reserving the natural pocket of the wing (if you are unsure of how to debone yourself, you can buy from the butcher and ask them to remove the bone for you)
vegetable oil, for deep-frying
approx. 200 g/1⅓ cups potato flour, for dusting
ponzu sauce (see page 151 or buy ready-made), for dipping

GYOZA FILLING
400 g/14 oz. minced/ground pork
1 tablespoon freshly grated ginger
1 teaspoon finely chopped garlic
1 tablespoon soy sauce
1 tablespoon mirin
1 red chilli/chile, finely chopped
a small bunch of coriander/cilantro, chopped
1 teaspoon table salt

Japanese bamboo steamer or regular vegetable steamer
deep-fat fryer or a large heavy-based pan suitable for deep-frying

MAKES 20 WINGS

Put all the gyoza filling ingredients into a large bowl and mix together.

Take a deboned chicken wing in one hand and gently place about 2 tablespoons of the stuffing mixture into the opening where the bone was, packing down gently between each addition. Pull the skin of the wing tight to neaten and make sure the filling is stuffed full. Fold over any flaps of meat or skin at the opening to secure the filling. Wrap the wing tightly in clingfilm/plastic wrap and repeat for the rest of the wings.

Preheat the water for the steamer. Place the wings (still in their plastic wrapping) in the steamer and steam for around 10 minutes; this may take longer depending on how many you cook at once or how big your steamer is. Check the wings are done by using a sharp knife to probe into the centre of the thickest wing for 5 seconds – if it comes out piping hot they are ready, if not carry on cooking until you achieve the desired temperature.

Allow the wings to cool, then remove the clingfilm/plastic wrap and transfer to the freezer uncovered for around 30 minutes to allow the chicken to dry on the outside, this will help them go really crispy when fried. You want to make them as cold as possible but not completely frozen, so transfer to the fridge after 30 minutes if not ready to start cooking.

When ready to cook, preheat the oil in a deep-fat fryer to 180°C (350°F) or fill a large heavy-based pan half-full with vegetable oil and heat until a cube of bread sizzles and rises to the surface instantly.

Dust the cold chicken wings in potato flour and deep-fry in small batches for around 5 minutes or until golden, turning halfway through. Remove the wings from the oil with a slotted spoon and place on paper towels to drain the excess oil. Ensure the wings are piping hot and serve straight away with ponzu sauce for dipping, if you like.

YAKITORI CHICKEN

Yakitori means grilled in Japanese, and these sticky-glazed skewers are popular finger food to be served as a snack or appetizer. They are also utterly delicious cooked on a barbecue/outdoor grill. I am using chicken for this recipe but you can use whatever you fancy really, salmon is also particularly good with this salty-sweet marinade. Dashi stock can be bought ready made or use my recipe on page 167.

10 skinless boneless chicken thighs
2 bunches of spring onions/scallions

YAKITORI MARINADE
180 ml/generous ¾ cup light soy sauce
150 ml/ ⅔ cup mirin
100 ml/⅓ cups plus 1 tablespoon sake
2½ tablespoons caster/granulated sugar
2 teaspoons salt
400 ml/scant 1¾ cups dashi stock (store-bought or see recipe page 167)

griddle pan/grill pan
10 metal or wooden barbecue skewers, soaked
baking sheet, lined with non-stick baking parchment

MAKES 10 SKEWERS

Dice the chicken thighs into 2-cm/¾-inch cubes and set aside in the fridge. Cut the spring onions/scallions into 5-cm/2-inch batons and also set these aside until required.

Place all the marinade ingredients in a saucepan, stir together and bring just to the boil. Remove from the heat and let cool. Once completely cool, place the chopped chicken and spring onion/scallion batons in the marinade and stir to give everything a good coating. Cover with clingfilm/plastic wrap and refrigerate for 2–3 hours.

When the time is up, remove the chicken and spring onion/scallion pieces from the marinade and thread five alternating pieces of chicken with four batons of spring onion/scallion onto each skewer. Transfer the leftover marinade into a saucepan and reduce over medium-high heat for 5–10 minutes to make a dipping sauce to serve with the skewers. Set this aside to cool until needed.

Preheat the oven to 180°C (350°F) Gas 4.

Preheat a griddle pan/grill pan over high heat until smoking hot. Carefully place the skewers into the hot pan with the end of each skewer hanging off the edge. Make sure you don't overcrowd the pan, you may well need to cook the chicken in two batches depending on the size of your pan. Cook the chicken until browned and caramelized on the outside, turning frequently. Transfer the skewers straight to the prepared baking sheet and bake in the preheated oven for around 10 minutes or until the meat is cooked through. Serve the skewers hot with the reduced marinade as a delicious dipping sauce.

HIRATA STEAMED PORK BUNS

This recipe for sticky caramelized pork belly inside soft bao buns is absolutely mouth-watering. It can be prepared in stages, if liked, and you can customize the filling by adding some pickled carrot or shavings of spring onion/scallion. Or mix up the filling all together and use slow-cooked beef or chicken instead. The perfect savoury precursor for any of the delicious sweet treats in this book.

HIRATA PORK BELLY
400-g/14-oz. piece pork belly
salt and pepper, to season
olive oil, for frying
3½ tablespoons each sake,
  mirin and soy sauce
4 teaspoons white sugar
500 ml/2 cups chicken stock
5 sancho peppercorns
1 star anise
1 whole dried chilli/chile

STEAMED BUNS
1 teaspoon dry active yeast
200 ml/1 cup warm water
450 g/scant 3½ cups plain/
  all-purpose flour
60 g/scant ⅓ cup caster/
  granulated sugar
¾ teaspoon baking powder
50 g/¼ cup double/heavy
  cream
sunflower oil, for brushing

BBQ KETCHUP
3 tablespoons vegetable oil
2 teaspoons each crushed
  garlic and grated ginger
125 ml/½ cup Shaoxing rice
  wine
3 tablespoons gochujang
  paste
70 g/⅓ cup white sugar
16–17 cherry tomatoes
3½ tablespoons oyster sauce
2½ tablespoons soy sauce
3½ tablespoons tamarind
  water
200 ml/¾–1 cup pork
  cooking liquid
freshly squeezed lime juice

DRESSED CUCUMBER
½ cucumber
100 ml/⅓ cup mirin
1 tablespoon white sugar
coriander/cilantro, to serve

stand mixer with a dough hook
10 squares of 10 x 10 cm/4 x
* 4 inch non-stick baking*
* parchment, greased*
bamboo or metal steamer
cook's blowtorch (optional)

To make the hirata pork belly, season the meat with salt and pepper and remove the rind. Preheat a little oil in a large, deep pan and sear the pork over high heat to caramelize the fat. Remove the meat from the pan and set aside. Add the sake to the hot pan and flame very carefully using a match. When the alcohol has burnt off, add the mirin, soy sauce and sugar and stir. Return the meat to the pan and cover with chicken stock. Add the peppercorns, star anise and chilli/chile. Cover and simmer gently for 3 hours (or cook in the oven at 140°C (280°F) Gas 1) until the meat is falling apart.

Remove the pork and sieve/strain the contents of the pan. Discard the aromatics and keep the liquid to use in the BBQ ketchup. Leave the pork to cool and then keep in the fridge until required.

To make the steamed buns, dissolve the yeast in the warm water and leave until frothy. Put all the other dough ingredients (apart from the oil) into the bowl of a stand mixer with the dough hook. Add the yeast water and knead with the dough hook for around 5 minutes until combined into a smooth dough. Transfer to a clean bowl and cover with clingfilm/plastic wrap. Rest in a warm place for 1 hour or until doubled in size.

Divide the risen dough into ten equal parts and roll each portion out on a lightly floured surface into small ovals, about the thickness and shape of a pitta bread. Fold each of these in half widthways and place onto the prepared squares of baking parchment on a baking sheet. Add a small piece of greased baking parchment to the fold of each bun to stop them sticking together at the fold. Brush the buns with the oil, cover the tray loosely with clingfilm/plastic wrap and leave in a warm place to rise for 15 minutes.

Preheat the water for the steamer. Use the parchment to transfer the buns to the steamer and cook for around 12 minutes. The steamer should not be overcrowded so you may need to do this in a few batches.

To make the BBQ ketchup, heat the oil in a frying pan/skillet and fry the garlic and ginger until fragrant. Deglaze the pan with the Shaoxing rice wine then stir in the gochujang paste and sugar. Cook for a few minutes until caramelized, then mix in all the remaining ingredients (apart from the lime juice). Cook for 5–10 minutes until reduced and the tomatoes have softened. Remove from the heat and pass through a sieve/strainer. Add a squeeze of lime juice to season and set aside to cool.

To make the cucumber, deseed and shred the cucumber. Boil the mirin and sugar with 3 tablespoons water. Mix with the cucumber and set aside.

To construct the buns, slice the pork belly into 2 cm/¾ inch thick slices. Heat a frying pan/skillet with a little oil and fry the pork slices over a medium-high heat for around 2 minutes on each side. Deglaze the pan with a little of the ketchup and turn off the heat. To give the buns a nice crisp finish use a cook's blowtorch to quickly sear the dough. Place a slice of pork in each bun with a little of the cucumber and some of the BBQ ketchup. Garnish with fresh coriander/cilantro and serve.

MAKES 10 BUNS

KAKIAGE PANCAKES

Kakiage pancakes are a very simple yet comforting and delicious street-food found all over Japan. They must be served freshly cooked to retain their crispness and the coating of batter only needs to be extremely light. I love to make these with a selection of vegetables but you can customize these with pretty much anything you like. Shellfish and fresh fish work extremely well, or even thin strips of lamb, chicken or beef. If using chicken, ensure it is cooked first.

PANCAKE BATTER
200 g/1½ cups self-raising/
    self-rising flour
200 g/2 cups cornflour/
    cornstarch
large pinch of salt, to season
approx. 400–500 ml/1¾–2
    cups very cold sparkling
    water

VEGETABLE FILLING
1 red onion
1 carrot
burdock root (or salsify
    is a nice alternative)
small bunch of spring onions/
    scallions
1 sweet potato
ponzu sauce (store-bought
    or see recipe page 151),
    for dipping

*deep-fat fryer or large pan
    suitable for deep-frying*

MAKES 10–15
SMALL PANCAKES

To make the pancake batter, put the dry ingredients into a large mixing bowl and slowly whisk in the very cold sparkling water until you get a nice smooth, thick pancake batter with a dropping consistency.

To make the vegetable filling, peel (as necessary) and slice your chosen vegetables into fine strips. Place the vegetables in a large bowl and mix with just enough batter to bind them all together.

Preheat the vegetable oil in a deep-fryer to 180°C (350°F) or fill a large heavy-based pan half-full with vegetable oil and heat until a cube of bread sizzles and rises to the surface instantly.

Dip a dessert spoon briefly into the hot oil then pick up a portion of the battered vegetables with the same spoon and drop it carefully into the fryer.

Cook a few pancakes at a time for approximately 2–3 minutes until golden, turning halfway. Remove with a slotted spoon and drain on paper towels. Repeat with the remaining batter and serve the hot pancakes immediately with ponzu sauce or an Asian dipping sauce of your choosing.

TAKOYAKI OCTOPUS DUMPLINGS FINISHED WITH KEWPIE & BULLDOG SAUCE

DASHI STOCK
100 g/3½ oz. bonito flakes, plus a few more for serving
100 g/3½ oz. dried dashi kombu kelp

DUMPLING BATTER
480 ml/generous 2 cups dashi stock (store-bought or see ingredients above)
2 eggs
1 teaspoon soy sauce
220 g/1⅔ cups plain/all-purpose flour
¼ teaspoon salt

DUMPLING FILLING
120 g/4¼ oz. fresh octopus, cleaned and cut into 2-cm/¾-inch cubes
2 teaspoons pickled red ginger (optional)
2 spring onions/scallions, thinly sliced

BULLDOG SAUCE
5 rounded tablespoons tomato ketchup
2 tablespoons Worcestershire sauce
1 tablespoon soy sauce
1 tablespoon mirin
4 teaspoons caster/granulated sugar
1 teaspoon Dijon mustard
½ garlic clove, grated

TO SERVE
kewpie mayonnaise
freshly chopped coriander/cilantro, to garnish

takoyaki pan or mini muffin pan, each hole brushed generously with sunflower oil to grease

MAKES 10 MINI PANCAKES

Takoyaki are traditional Japanese street-food dumplings – usually served with octopus and made in a special takoyaki pan, which you can buy online and in specialist Japanese stores. You can make these in a mini muffin pan in the oven instead, but I find that cooking over the stove gives the best texture and flavour. The batter is loosely similar to that of a Yorkshire pudding. If you don't want to use octopus, you could make these with small shrimp or extra vegetables instead. Kewpie mayonnaise is a delicious Japanese condiment with a rich, sweet, umami edge, the leftovers from this recipe go beautifully with many other dishes. The dashi stock will make more than you need but keeps well in the fridge for 2–3 days.

If you are making the dashi stock, bring 900 ml/4 cups minus 1½ tablespoons water to the boil. Add the bonito flakes and kombu kelp and boil together for 2 minutes. Remove from the heat, let cool and then strain the stock, discarding the contents of the sieve/strainer.

To make the dumpling batter, put 480 ml/generous 2 cups of cold dashi stock, the eggs and soy sauce in a bowl and whisk together. Whisk in the flour and salt until fully combined into a smooth, thick batter. Pour the batter into a jug/pitcher and set aside for a moment.

To make the bulldog sauce, simply mix together all the ingredients until fully combined. Set aside for serving later.

To make the dumplings, set the greased takoyaki pan directly over medium heat. When the pan is smoking hot, pour batter to each hole, filling right to the top. Carefully and fairly quickly place a cube of octopus, a few strands of pickled red ginger and a strand of spring onion/scallion in the centre of each dumpling before the batter has time to set. Prod down gently using a spoon.

After about 5 minutes and as the dumplings start to colour, gently turn them over using a spoon. Be careful as the dumplings and the pan will be hot. (Alternatively, you can cook these in a mini muffin pan in a hot oven for about 15 minutes.) When the dumplings are golden brown all over, remove from the pan making sure the octopus in the centre is piping hot.

To construct the dish, serve the dumplings hot on a large serving dish drizzled generously with kewpie mayonnaise and bulldog sauce. Sprinkle over some bonito flakes and chopped coriander/cilantro to garnish.

PANKO DOUGHNUTS STUFFED WITH PORK KATSU

Everyone knows that a good doughnut can get you through the toughest of days, and these are no exception. The concept of a savoury doughnut may seem unusual to the Western palate but actually, savoury doughnuts have been around for a long time in Japan and are appearing on Western menus as the trend for fusion street-food spreads. Savoury stuffed breads are a regular at Japanese-French fusion pâtisseries. They make the most delicious snack, trust me, once you bite through the hot, crispy coating to the slightly sweet soft dough and beneath to the sticky curry-glazed pork stuffing, you will forever be craving another one! Leftover katsu sauce will keep in the fridge up to 5 days to be used in another meal.

DOUGHNUT DOUGH

30 g/1 oz. fresh yeast or
   15 g/2½ teaspoons instant
   dried yeast
450 g/scant 3¼ cups white/
   strong bread flour
1 heaped teaspoon salt
45 g/scant ¼ cup sugar
200 ml/generous ¾ cup
   warm water
30 g/1 oz. lightly beaten egg
   (approx. ½ egg)
45 g/3¼ tablespoons butter,
   melted
vegetable oil, for deep-frying

PORK KATSU FILLING

1½ tablespoons butter
½ small onion, chopped
1 garlic clove, chopped
50 g/½ cup peeled and finely
   chopped cooking apple
   (such as Bramley apple)

To make the doughnut dough, if using fresh yeast, dissolve the yeast in 20 ml/4 teaspoons warm water taken from the 200 ml/generous ¾ cup. Leave for 10 minutes until frothy.

Meanwhile, mix together the flour, salt and sugar in the bowl of a stand mixer fitted with a dough hook (or a large mixing bowl). If using instant dried yeast, add this to the bowl now along with the 200 ml/generous ¾ cup warm water. Or add the dissolved fresh yeast with the remaining warm water. Add the lightly beaten egg and knead by hand or with the dough hook to bring the dough together – it should be soft and smooth so add a little more water if required.

Add the melted butter and continue to knead for 10 minutes until soft and stretchy (see **A**, overleaf). Put the dough in a lightly oiled bowl and cover with clingfilm/plastic wrap. Leave for 1 hour in a warm place to rise.

Divide the dough into ten equal portions of around 40 g/1½ oz. each and shape into smooth round balls. Place each ball of dough on a greased square of baking parchment and arrange on a tray (see **B**, overleaf). Cover the tray loosely with greased clingfilm/plastic wrap and leave in a warm place to rise again for 45–60 minutes or until doubled in size.

When the dough has risen, preheat the oil in a deep-fryer to 180°C (350°F) or fill a large heavy-based pan half-full with vegetable oil and heat until a cube of bread sizzles and rises to the surface instantly.

Carefully slide the doughnuts, still on the baking parchment, into the hot oil – the paper will float to the surface and can then be removed. You will probably need to fry in batches of three or four depending on the size of your pan. Cook for around 3 minutes and use a slotted spoon to turn when the middle becomes golden brown. Fry until an even colour is achieved on both sides. Remove the doughnuts from the pan with the slotted spoon and drain the excess oil on paper towels. Set aside.

continued overleaf

A

B

C

D

½ teaspoon ground turmeric
1 teaspoon medium strength
   curry powder
300 ml/generous 1¼ cups
   chicken stock
100 ml/generous ⅓ cup
   coconut milk
1 tablespoon runny honey
1 tablespoon vegetable oil
250 g/9 oz. minced/ground
   pork
salt and black pepper,
   to taste

CRISPY PANKO COATING
4 eggs, lightly beaten
approx. 200 g/1½ cups plain/
   all-purpose flour
approx. 200 g/4⅔ cups
   panko breadcrumbs

ten 8 x 8-cm/3½ x 3½-inch
   squares of baking
   parchment, greased with
   oil spray
deep-fat fryer or a large pan
   suitable for deep-frying

MAKES 10 DOUGHNUTS

To make the pork katsu filling, place the butter, chopped onion and garlic in a saucepan and cook until the onion softens. Add the apple and cook, stirring, for a further three minutes. Mix in the turmeric and curry powder, then pour in the chicken stock and coconut milk. Stir together and simmer the sauce over high heat for approximately 12–15 minutes until thickened. Add the honey, then season to taste with salt and pepper and remove from the heat and set aside for a moment.

Preheat a large frying pan/skillet or wok and add the vegetable oil. Stir-fry the minced/ground pork quickly over a high heat until golden in colour. Season the meat to taste and then add a few tablespoons of the katsu sauce and stir to de-glaze the pan. The pork should then be sticky and glazed with the sauce. Set aside ready for filling the doughnuts.

To make the crispy panko coating, ready the beaten egg, flour and panko breadcrumbs in three separate dishes or containers. Using a small sharp knife, cut a hole in the centre of each doughnut. Stuff each with a couple of spoonfuls of the pork katsu mixture **(C)** then roll in the flour, followed by the beaten egg and finally the panko breadcrumbs **(D)**. Make sure the doughnuts are completely covered in breadcrumbs (especially the opening with the stuffing) and then repeat the flour, egg and breadcrumb coating process once more.

Preheat the same cooking oil in a deep-fryer or pan to 180°C (350°F) or heat until a cube of bread sizzles and rises to the surface instantly.

Return the doughnuts to the fryer in small batches and cook (turning half-way) until the breadcrumbs are nice and golden all the way around. Remove from the oil with a slotted spoon and drain the excess oil on paper towels. Serve the doughnuts warm.

VARIATION
For a delicious vegetarian alternative, I would recommend a combination of finely diced shallots, mushrooms, carrots and leeks, all sweated together in a pan until tender. Add this mixture to the katsu sauce instead of the pork.

TONKOTSU PORK FINGERS WITH APPLE & CHERRY BLOSSOM PURÉE

PORK FILLING
olive oil, for frying
400 g/14 oz. pork shoulder, diced and seasoned with salt and pepper
3½ tablespoons each sake, mirin and soy sauce
4 teaspoons caster/granulated sugar
500 ml/2 cups plus 2 tablespoons chicken stock
1 star anise
5 sansho peppercorns
1 whole dried chilli/chile

APPLE & CHERRY BLOSSOM PURÉE
2 cooking apples (such as Bramley, peeled, cored and diced)
freshly squeezed juice of ½ lemon
a knob/pat of butter
3¼ tablespoons white sugar
salt, to season
1–2 teaspoons cherry blossom flavouring, to taste (optional)

CRISPY COATING
2 eggs, lightly beaten
200 g/1½ cups plain/all-purpose flour
200 g/4⅔ cups panko breadcrumbs
1 sheet of dry nori seaweed, ground to a fine powder
olive oil, for frying

flat-bottomed loaf pan, square/rectangle pan or plastic container, lined with clingfilm/plastic wrap, for pressing the meat
baking sheet, lined with non-stick baking parchment

MAKES 20 PORK FINGERS

A true crowd-pleaser – juicy confit pork is compressed and fried in a crispy coating spiked with seaweed. It is best to make the filling the day before to allow time for it to set, 2 hours is the minimum.

To make the pork filling, preheat a little oil in a large, deep pan and sear the pork over high heat to caramelize the fat. Remove the meat from the pan and set aside. Add the sake to the hot pan and flame very carefully using a match. When the alcohol has burnt off, stir in the mirin, soy sauce and sugar. Return the meat to the pan and cover with chicken stock. Add the star anise, peppercorns and chilli/chile. Cover and simmer gently for 3 hours (or cook in the oven at 140°C (280°F) Gas 1) until the meat is falling apart.

Remove the pork and strain the contents of the pan. Discard the aromatics, keeping the liquid. Let the pork cool and refrigerate until needed.

Return the cooking liquid to the pan and set over medium heat until reduced to a thick syrup; around 5–10 minutes. Meanwhile, roughly shred the meat with your fingers or with a fork, not too finely. When the cooking liquid has reduced, mix a little through to lightly dress the meat – if too wet it will make the crispy coating soggy. Press the meat into the prepared pan, packing it firmly down. Cover with clingfilm/plastic wrap and place in the fridge to chill and set for a minimum of 2 hours or ideally overnight.

To make the apple and cherry blossom purée, put the apples in a small heavy-based saucepan and add the lemon juice, butter and sugar. Cook over low-medium heat for 15–20 minutes until the apples are completely soft. Allow to cool and then blitz with a hand blender until smooth. Season with salt and add cherry blossom flavouring to taste. Set aside until needed.

To construct the pork fingers, remove the pork from the mould using the layer of clingfilm/plastic wrap underneath. Discard the clingfilm/plastic wrap and cut the compressed meat to your chosen size fingers. I have gone for 8 x 2 cm/3 x ¾ inch rectangles but you can make them as preferred. Put the beaten egg, flour and breadcrumbs in three separate dishes. Mix the ground nori into the breadcrumbs. Roll the pork fingers one by one in the flour, egg and finally the breadcrumbs, until evenly coated.

Preheat the oven to 200°C (400°F) Gas 6.

Put enough oil in a large frying pan/skillet to coat the base and preheat to 180°C (350°F). Shallow-fry the pork fingers, until the breadcrumbs are golden – you may well need to do this in a few batches so as not to overcrowd the pan. Drain the excess oil on paper towels. Transfer to the prepared baking sheet and bake in the preheated oven for around 5–10 minutes. A knife pierced into the centre of the pork for 5 seconds should feel piping hot. Serve with the apple and cherry blossom purée for dipping.

INDEX

SUPPLIERS

Below is a list of trusted suppliers for specialist ingredients and equipment used throughout this book. I hope it will help you on your way to making some fantastic pâtisserie.

SILIKOMART MOULDS
I would like to take this opportunity to thank the great people at Silikomart, all the incredible silicone moulds I have used for this book were very generously donated by this amazing company. I have used their innovative products many times throughout my career because, in my opinion, they are the best in the business. www.silikomart.com. The moulds I have used from Silikomart in this book are as follows: p.34 Pillow, p.74 Kit Red Tail, p.82 Stella Del Circo, p. 86 Vague, p.90 Gianduia, p.94 Eclipse, p.96 Modular Flex Wave.

THE JAPAN CENTRE
A brilliant Japanese supermarket based in central London. They also deliver within the UK and Europe.
www.japancentre.com

RITTER COURIVAUD
Supplier of top quality specialist ingredients from all around the world. Including chocolate and cocoa fat colouring and decorative ingredients such as silver and gold leaf and lustre powders.
www.rittercourivaud.co.uk

MSK INGREDIENTS
Fantastic online speciality pâtisserie supplier. Great for professional grade food colourings, all things molecular gastronomy (including spherification kits) and finishing touches.
www.msk-ingredients.com

HOME CHOCOLATE FACTORY
A UK supplier of SOSA products (leading manufacturers of premium ingredients for pastry chefs and bakers).
www.homechocolatefactory.com

ACKNOWLEDGEMENTS

Thank you to all the amazing chefs I have worked with, who have inspired me throughout my career: Gary Rhodes, Wayne Tapsfield, David Nicholls and Lisa Phillips to name but a few. To Suzy, Evie and Oliver. To my amazing family and friends. To Alex Laverick and the incredibly talented Jon Jones, without whom this book would not have been possible. To Mowie and Tony, who brought my recipes to life with beautiful props and stunning photography. Thank you to Megan, Alice, Julia, Leslie and the rest of the team at Ryland Peters & Small who helped to make this book a success. To everyone who has supported me and believed in me throughout my career: Thank you. This book is for you.

Ryland Peters & Small would like to thank:

THE WASABI COMPANY
For the kind donation of specialist Japanese ingredients for the photography
www.thewasabicompany.co.uk

'I have known James Campbell for over 15 years. James joined me as Pastry Chef at the Mandarin Oriental in London after being recommended to me by my good friend Gary Rhodes. James was previously Gary's Pastry Chef in his Michelin starred restaurant and James wanted to branch out to a larger operation with more diversity. It was an excellent decision to employ James, he is a very talented Pastry Chef, an extremely good leader, teacher, mentor and above all a great person. After working for me for six years, James decided that the time was right to move on to new horizons. Still driven by producing top quality food but looking more at the mass market and commercial side of the industry, he joined M&S. He has clearly continued to grow in his new position and I am delighted to see his advancement. Along with his work, James is also a dedicated family man. Even with these commitments he still makes time to support me with my charity and is involved in annual fundraising activities. I wish James the very best of luck and success with this book. If James has had a hand in it, I am certain that it will be a great book, the recipes are sure to produce quality desserts and pastries, and I would encourage everyone to purchase it.'

DAVID NICHOLLS, GLOBAL DIRECTOR OF FOOD AND BEVERAGE AT THE MANDARIN ORIENTAL HOTELS